SADAKICHI HARTMANN

SADAKICHI HARTMANN

MEMENTO

Collected Poems, 1886–1944
edited by Floyd Cheung

LITTLE ISLAND PRESS

Lodgemore Lane,
Stroud, GL5 3EQ

Published in the United Kingdom by
Little Island Press, Stroud

Introductory and editorial material
© Floyd Cheung 2016

Image on p.6: 'Sadakichi Hartmann' by Cliff
Wesselmann. (From the Holdings of Special
Collections & Archives, UCR Libraries,
University of California, Riverside)

First Published 2016

ISBN 978–0–9935056–2–1

Design & Typesetting by t.r.u
typographic research unit

Typeset in Bembo MT

CONTENTS

'Sadakichi is singular, never plural', declared Gertrude Stein. Indeed, there can have been only one Carl Sadakichi Hartmann (1867–1944). An innovative writer, critic, performer and bon vivant extraordinaire, Hartmann helped to introduce Japanese poetic forms to the English literary tradition, championed photography as an art form, conducted 'concerts' with smells instead of sounds, and drank riotously with everyone from the Symbolist poets of Paris to the Bohemians of Greenwich Village to the movie stars of Hollywood.[1] Yet this singular figure wore many masks. For instance, Hartmann wrote under several pseudonyms. Besides using his birth name (though omitting 'Carl' to balance his biracial heritage between 'Sadakichi' and 'Hartmann'), he published as 'Sidney Allan', 'Caliban', 'Hogarth', 'Juvenal', 'Innocent De Salle', 'Chrysanthemum', and even 'A. Chameleon'. Sometimes, two personae appeared side by side in the same publication.

Hartmann could read, write, and speak English, French, and German, though not Japanese. He made up for his lack of Japanese language, however, with his performance abilities and striking physiognomy. Referring to his biracial heritage, a friend called him 'a living freak presumably sired by Mephistopheles out of Madame Butterfly'.[2] Hartmann even played the court magician in Douglas Fairbanks' film *The Thief of Bagdad* (1924). Throughout his life, he secured speaking engagements – billing himself sometimes as Sadakichi and other times as Allan. When lecturing on a Japanese topic, Hartmann donned a kimono. When a more sober, less racially marked persona was required, he wore a suit. Although he liked saying, 'I personally never think of myself as a German or Asiatic. Others do it for me', he clearly knew how to modulate his mixed-race ancestry for different audiences and purposes.[3] Hartmann understood the significance of the newly coined concept 'Eurasian', and saw that the turn of the twentieth century might be a good moment for his emergence as a singular personality with plural aspects.[4]

Born in 1867 on the isle of Dejima, Japan, to a Prussian merchant named Carl Herman Oskar Hartmann and a Japanese woman named Osada, the young Hartmann was sent to be raised by a rich uncle in Hamburg after his mother died a few months after his birth.[5] Baptized a Lutheran and wrapped in luxury, Hartmann learned literature, art, and upper-class deportment during his childhood. Being forced to attend the German Imperial Naval Academy, however, did not agree with the independent-minded, teenaged Hartmann, who decamped to Paris. Displeased, his father shipped him off to another branch of his family in Philadelphia in 1882 with $3 in pocket money. The already melancholy Hartmann keenly felt this change of scene, especially since he had to work sometimes as a lithographic stippler, perfume peddler, photographic retoucher, or spittoon cleaner. For solace, he turned to books. In Germany, he had devoured European classics like Victor Hugo's *Les Miserables* whose main character Hartmann considered more of a father figure than his biological father.[6]

In Philadelphia, Hartmann continued to read voraciously in libraries and bookstores, eventually discovering *Leaves of Grass* by Walt Whitman. Thoroughly taken with Whitman's verse, he visited him in Camden, New Jersey, in 1884, starting what would become a deep if tumultuous relationship. In addition, via multiple cross-country trips, visits to Europe, and correspondence, Hartmann came to know many other writers including Stéphane Mallarmé,

Paul Verlaine, Ezra Pound, George Santayana, and of course Gertrude Stein.

Disowned by his father and searching for a mentor, the seventeen-year-old Hartmann sought out the sixty-five-year-old Whitman to learn both about poetry and how to be a poet. From 1884 until 1891, Hartmann visited Whitman often. They cooked, ate, talked, and read each other's drafts. In an early poem, Hartmann expressed his appreciation: 'I am bound to thee forever, thy works were to me, except Love and Nature, the grandest lessons of my life.'[7] Although Hartmann sometimes embarrassed Whitman by telling tales out of school, inciting the latter to call the former 'that damned Japanee', Whitman still believed in him: 'I have more hopes of him, more faith in him than any of the boys.' Whitman knew other aspiring poets of Japanese ancestry, like Yone Noguchi, but he apparently admired Hartmann most of all.[8]

Whitman served as a model for Hartmann's literary career, although it was not so much that the young poet imitated the old master's style, suggests George Knox and Harry W. Lawton, but that Whitman 'influenced the literary pose which Hartmann adopted toward the world'. Specifically, they argue, Hartmann adopted 'Whitman's techniques of self-promotion, a belief in democracy despite his tendency toward seeing art as primarily for the elite, the use of press-agentry methods pioneered by Whitman, and an assertive Bohemianism traceable to Whitman.'[9]

Hartmann's early poems do, however, bear traces of Whitman's stylistic influence. For instance, Hartmann was inspired by Whitman's frequent use of natural and nautical images even if he did not couch them in free verse or anaphora. For instance, Hartmann borrows visions of waves and sails from Whitman's 'Sea-Drift' poems, and

Whitman's *Leaves of Grass* is echoed in the title of his *Drifting Flowers of the Sea and Other Poems*. Images of individual leaves of grass and flowers floating on water evoke the natural, the small, the down-to-earth. But unlike Whitman's rooted and perennial grass, Hartmann's flowers drift and fade. Whitman's speaker assures his readers at the end of 'Song of Myself':

I bequeath myself to the dirt to grow from the grass I love,
If you want me again look for me under your boot-soles.
…
I stop somewhere waiting for you.[10]

Hartmann's ideology of flowers, in contrast, is informed by the Japanese concept of *mono no aware*, which he translated as 'the fugitiveness of all earthly things'.[11] Natural beauty derives partly from its impermanence. In the opening poem of *Drifting Flowers,* 'Nocturne', the speaker repeatedly conjures images of waves and sails and the melodies of 'lovers' lays', each rising in its beautiful moment and then 'lost in the dim unknown'. Seven chain-rhymed quatrains precede a sestet in which earlier phrases return before they fade away. Even the poem's use of indentation suggests a fading away into the distance. One quatrain looks like this on the page:

Sails gleam and glimmer ghostly white,
   They come and slowly drift away,
      Lost in the monotone of night,
         Like visions of a summer-day.

Hence, at least some of Hartmann's early poems share Whitman's vocabulary of images if not his confidence in perennial return.

10

As 'Nocturne' suggests, Hartmann saw beauty in this world as transient. It comes and drifts away. He applied this view also to life and personal relationships. In an essay he wrote for *The Papyrus* called 'The Solitary Horseman', Hartmann asks, 'are we mortals not all wayfarers in time and space?' and answers, 'we pursue our journey along the highways of life – friend after friend being left on the wayside and hope after hope carried away by the wind, until at last our soul, freed from its earthly tenement, drifts through space like a whirling leaf.'

In 1891, after a bout of severe depression, Hartmann attempted to free his own soul from its earthly tenement. During his recovery, he met and married his nurse, Elizabeth Blanche Walsh, to whom he dedicated *Drifting Flowers*. They thrived for a while. In 1892, she witnessed his naturalization as a US citizen, and the 1900 census lists their residence in New York with him as the head of a household that included her as well as four children.[12] Yet by the time the first manuscript edition of *Drifting Flowers* was released in 1904, their marriage was falling apart. Two poems that appeared together on the third page attest to Hartmann's transient view of romantic relationships. In 'Why I Love Thee?' the speaker answers that one might as well 'Ask why the seawind wanders'. In 'Why I No Longer Love Thee?' the speaker points out that the 'summer has fled'. The 'seafaring ships' of the first poem find themselves 'wrecked on the ashen strand' of the second. This language suggests that love comes and goes as seasons change, tides ebb and flow, and ships sail and sometimes sink. Hence, Hartmann borrowed often from Whitman's bank of natural and nautical imagery, but he tended to color them with *mono no aware*.

Similarly, Hartmann's title poem 'Drifting Flowers of the Sea' owes much to Whitman's 'As I Ebb'd with the

Ocean of Life', but again the differences are telling (beyond the former's use of rhyme and regular meter and the latter's choice of anaphoric free verse). Whitman's second stanza begins:

As I wend to the shores I know not,
As I list to the dirge, the voices of men and women wreck'd,
As I inhale the impalpable breezes that set in upon me,
As the ocean so mysterious rolls toward me closer and closer,
I too but signify at the utmost a little wash'd-up drift,
A few sands and dead leaves to gather,
Gather, and merge myself as part of the sands and drift.[13]

Here we find familiar Whitmanian techniques and tropes: the repetition, a beach setting, and a merging of the self and nature. In Hartmann's poem, the speaker also finds himself inhaling shore-line scents:

The pungent smell of the seaweed strays –
  From vast and trackless spaces
    Where wind and water meet,
      White flowers, that rise from the sleepless deep,
        Come drifting to my feet.

But instead of Whitman's dead leaves, ethereal white flowers gather on the shore. Hartmann's water-borne flowers may or may not conjure the image of Asian lotus blossoms or water lilies. The fact that they emerge from 'the sleepless deep', however, suggests that their origin is otherworldly, perhaps in the speaker's psyche. This is confirmed in the second stanza as the poem takes us from simile to metaphor. The white flowers are not only 'Like dreams of love' but also 'the songs […] I dreamt but never sung … /

12

Pale hopes my thoughts alone have known, / Vain words ne'er uttered'. Hence, while Whitman's speaker identifies as one with the 'drift and debris', Hartmann's speaker sees the drifting flowers as signs of unexpressed desire. And in the end these thought-flowers, safe in their psychological vault, endure the apocalypse of this world 'when the bell of time will ring the doom' in order to 'rise in fugitive bloom' on the shores of another world.

Whereas 'As I Ebb'd' might be termed Transcendental in its monism regarding the speaker's unity with nature, Hartmann's 'Drifting Flowers' can be considered Symbolist in its use of an image to enable transport to an alternate state of being. As Kirsten Blythe Painter explains, Symbolists like Mallarmé and Verlaine conceive of 'ultimate reality as a realm beyond space and time'. They seek access via their poetry to two different spheres: 'the higher sphere of the mystical beyond and the inner sphere of the self.' They could accomplish this poetically by employing images of 'concrete things of the everyday world … as vehicles to the unseen.'[14] Hartmann married this poetic philosophical stance with Whitmanian imagery and Japanese aesthetics.

From the Symbolists, Hartmann also learned how to elicit and mix sensory experiences in his poetry. Writers like Mallarmé and Verlaine believed that synesthesia – the evocation of one sense via the stimulus of another (e.g., hearing the color blue) – 'sometimes allows the poet access to an infinite, mysterious space beyond this world'.[15] Consider, for instance, Hartmann's 'Cyanogen Seas Are Surging' from *Naked Ghosts*. Readers are meant to see, hear, and smell lines like 'Cyanogen seas are surging / On fierce cinnabarine strands'. The first part of the first word in this line reminds us of the color cyan, which initiates a visual experience that quickly turns to smell once we recall that cyanogen is a gas with an almond-like odor, and the bright red of mercuric cinnabar may inspire the smell and taste of cinnamon as well by aural association. The sibilance of the words *cyanogen*, *seas*, *surging*, *fierce*, *cinnabarine*, and *strands* further blends their sounds and meanings together. For Hartmann, the sound is as important as the sense. The synesthesia and heady word play serve to transport the speaker to another world.

Hartmann believed that his contemporaries did not pay enough attention to the sense of smell in particular. In one book, he reminds his readers that when the character Ulysses returns to Greece disguised as a beggar, his dog recognizes him: 'Undoubtedly by smell. And does not smell constitute a notable (in human beings neglected and unconscious) part of memory?'[16] To demonstrate the potential of smell to transport an audience, Hartmann conducted a 'Perfume Concert' in 1902 with the aid of giant electric fans. He planned to take his audience on 'A Trip to Japan in Sixteen Minutes' with eight scents.[17] Alas, a lack of technological advancement and audience patience doomed his performance, and he was booed off stage. The experimental and audacious quality of this attempt, however, attests to Hartmann's fearlessness and imagination as an artist.

In fact, Hartmann cultivated an intense interest in art because of its ability to transport maker and audience to other worlds – inner and outer. He practiced many arts from dancing to acting to painting and, of course, writing. At the same time, he emerged as one of his era's great art critics. Jane Calhoun Weaver observes that 'few writers were as important to the art of the United States at the end of the nineteenth century and beginning of the twentieth as Sadakichi Hartmann.' She makes the point that 'a reading of the 1890–1915 era in American art is virtually impossible without recourse to Hartmann's writings.'[18]

In an essay entitled 'On the Vanity of Appreciation', Hartmann argued that 'true artists' are likely to live in poverty and obscurity, since they avoid pandering to commercial demands and rarely gain recognition for their work during their lifetimes. Art critics might help a few worthy artists, but 'art criticism,' Hartmann emphasized, 'is to me nothing but a peculiar mania for searching every expression of art, and life as well, for its most individual, perhaps innermost, essence.'[19] Thus, pursuing art and art criticism for Hartmann was primarily a way of life – not a way of making a living, though he did have to find paying work to support himself and his families.[20]

Fortunately Alfred Stieglitz recognized Hartmann as an especially articulate and discerning critic of photography and hired him to write for his journals, *Camera Notes* and *Camera Work*. Each issue featured reproductions of prints by leading pictorialist photographers of the day like Gertrude Käsebier, Eduard Steichen, and Steiglitz himself. Hartmann contributed essays on photography, reviews of art exhibitions, and poems to accompany these prints. In essays, he praised photographers like Steichen for having the 'courage to experiment and the ambition to break with conventional laws and to create new formulae of expression.'[21] In poems like 'Dawn-Flowers', which responds to Steichen's work of the same name, Hartmann transports readers to 'the land of shadows and dreams'.

Even as Hartmann sought the otherworldly in many of his early poems and through fine art, he thoroughly enjoyed life in this world. In *Passport to Immortality*, he claimed, 'Life … is a frolicsome farce to enjoy and laugh at … Tra-la-la!'[22] When not sick from asthma, he revelled in his body

15

by traveling, dancing, making love, gardening, and drinking. The latter activity he called his 'everyday moistening process'.[23] Hartmann enjoyed life so much that he earned the title of 'King of Bohemia' during his time and was retrospectively considered 'The First Hippie' in the 1960s.[24] In addition, he advocated that photographers consider everyday street scenes as worthy of their attention.[25] He admired, for instance, Stieglitz's photograph of the Flatiron Building in New York and even wrote his own poem 'To the "Flat Iron"', in which he called the edifice 'Rich, in showing no pretence, / Fair, in frugalness sublime'. Although Hartmann grew up in Hamburg and retired in California, he made New York the playground of his prime. There he kept all hours and lived every moment to its fullest.

II

For Hartmann and many other turn-of-the-century Americans, a translated Persian twelfth-century work captured the carpe diem spirit of their age: Edward FitzGerald's English version of *The Rubaiyat of Omar Khayyám*. The long poem features, for instance, the famous quatrain:

A Book of Verses underneath the Bough,
A Jug of Wine, a Loaf of Bread – and Thou
Beside me singing in the Wilderness –
Oh, Wilderness were Paradise enow![26]

FitzGerald's five editions of Khayyám's poem from 1859 to 1889 set off an 'Omar craze' and inspired many imitators.[27]

Written in 1913 and revised in 1916, during the height of World War I, Hartmann's *My Rubaiyat* critiques war profiteering and encourages its audience to seize the day

16

by refusing to bear arms. In the first stanza gray skies loom over a fading garden. While one critic identifies the pathetic fallacy at work here, Hartmann's speaker emphasizes the societal causes of this dreary condition.[28] In order to rid themselves of undesirable plants, people have filled the air with 'Smoke of weed-fires'. That is, people have polluted the environment; nature is not merely reflecting human emotion. In stanza thirty-three, the speaker observes, 'Smoke dragons coil 'round culm and stack / And belch foul breath into the street'. Military and industrial complexes may lead to profit for a few, but they choke the many. Similarly, in a book entitled *Permanent Peace: Is it a Dream?* Hartmann claimed, 'wars are invariably fought for strictly material reasons'.[29] *My Rubaiyat* critiques the 'greed' of a few and then calls for general draft resistance: 'If young and old refused to bear / Arms 'gainst brethren they do not know, / Then only, in some dim future / May we greet the dawn-doves of peace.' Although Hartmann usually avoided politics, his writing sometimes demonstrated a commitment to cultural critique that also led him to help Emma Goldman found the journal *Mother Earth*, which articulated a strong anti-war stance.

In his prefatory remarks to the third revised edition, Hartmann admits that his poem is a work in progress. He states that 'a poem of the scope and range of *My Rubaiyat* is never complete.' He thus took his cue from Walt Whitman who revised *Leaves of Grass* at least six times, but Hartmann admitted that his work could not match the 'word music' of Whitman's masterpiece. In addition, he conceded that *My Rubaiyat* 'is too didactic'. In the same set of remarks, however, Hartmann identified the strengths of his poetic techniques: subtlety of rhythm, concentration of image, and 'pictorial suggestion'. These techniques, he said, could be found also in Japanese poetry. Hence, *My Rubaiyat* may have enabled Hartmann to join the 'Omar craze' and reach his intended audience of 'chambermaids as well as cognoscenti, ordinary business men as well as solitary artistic souls', but the forms that may have suited his poetic strengths best were Japanese in origin.

Hartmann had written in Japanese forms like the haiku, tanka, and dodoitsu since at least 1898.[30] In 1904, he included seven tanka in *Drifting Flowers of the Sea and Other Poems.* Guido Bruno published a chapbook of his haiku and tanka in 1915, and in 1926, Hartmann produced a limited edition of one hundred mimeographed copies of *Japanese Rhythms,* which included haiku and tanka as well as three dodoitsu. He expanded this work once more in 1933. In his editorial comments, Hartmann described tanka as a 'short poem … the most popular and characteristic of the various forms of Japanese poetry. It consists of 5, 7, 5, 7, and 7 syllables – 31 in all.' Using an older spelling of haiku, Hartmann explained, 'The Haikai is a Tanka minus the concluding fourteen syllables.' And finally, 'The Dodoitsu is a more common and lawless form of poetical expression, limited to four lines of 7, 7, 7, and 5 syllables.' It is important to note that the non-Japanese speaking Hartmann equated what the Japanese call a unit of sound or *on* with what he understood as a syllable. In some cases, words match syllable for *on* and some do not. For example, in English the word *Nippon* is pronounced with two syllables, but in Japanese four *on* are required. Hence many contemporary writers of haiku in English choose to use fewer than seventeen syllables and may even print their work in a single line to capture what seems to them a truer sense of the brevity and single-breath recitability of Japanese-language haiku. Hartmann, however, was a pioneer of an older style of writing English-language poems inspired by Japanese forms.

Besides helping to regularize seventeen-syllable, three-line haiku in English, Hartmann employed end-rhyme, a technique that he practiced in most of his other poetry. In 1904, he claimed, 'The addition of rhyme is original with the author.' Critic Deckard Francis Hodge observes that Hartmann's formal choice constricts his range of diction.[31] Hartmann explained in 1926, however, 'The addition of rhyme was considered essential for subtler idiomatic and stylistic interpretation', as is shown in the following tanka:

'Though Love has grown cold
The woods are bright with flowers,
    Why not as of old
Go to the wildwood bowers
And dream of – bygone hours!

Here Hartmann's Japanese form meets Western allusion and idiom, which are emphasized by the end-rhyming of *flowers*, *bowers*, and *hours*. Retreat to a bower may have triggered readers to remember Samuel Taylor Coleridge's 'This Lime-Tree Bower My Prison' (1797), a classic poem. 'Bygone hours' would have struck turn-of-the-twentieth-century readers as slightly dated but still idiomatic, appropriate for a poem about the ways 'of old'. Hence Hartmann may have sacrificed some poetic freedom, but he gained access to a whole tradition. Hodge rightly notes that Hartmann's tanka and haiku 'reveal a playfulness in regard to boundaries, an acknowledgement of their existence, but also a willingness to traverse them.'[32] Indeed, Hartmann served as a crucial bridge across literary boundaries, a 'missing link' of American poetry – between Whitman and Pound, Japan and America, the nineteenth and the twentieth centuries.[33]

Hartmann's popularization of Japanese forms had a substantial impact on the development of modern American poetry. In particular, Hartmann valued concentration of image and 'pictorial suggestion', which were associated with Japanese poetics and would come to be thought of as Modernist. Other emergent poets of his day, many with whom Hartmann talked and corresponded, also valued these qualities. Poets like Ezra Pound and Amy Lowell searched for alternatives to what they considered the unnecessary ornateness and length of most Victorian poetry. Whereas Lowell modelled her work after ancient Greek and Latin examples, Pound found inspiration in Chinese and Japanese precedents. Together, they and others articulated the aesthetics of the Imagist movement. As Pound wrote in 1914, 'The image is itself the speech. The image is the word beyond formulated language … The Japanese … have understood the beauty of this sort of knowing.'[34]

How did Pound learn Japanese epistemology? Literary historian Ce Rosenow explains, 'Pound knew Hartmann and Hartmann's persona, which, perhaps more than his written work, contributed to Pound's understanding of Japan.'[35] Whether Pound read Hartmann's poems is unknown, but as interested as he was in Japanese poetics, one imagines that he may have come across Hartmann's 1904 essay 'The Japanese Conception of Poetry' published in *Reader Magazine*. In this piece Hartmann describes the Japanese aesthetic of suggestiveness, which requires readers to concentrate on an image and make their own epistemological connections. For example, Hartmann explains that a Japanese poet 'simply depicts a crow sitting on a withered branch, and leaves it to the reader to complete the poetic thought'.[36] The image itself is the speech, as Pound would say ten years later. Referring to his own poetry, Hartmann claims, 'Lines like "turn phantoms with the colder morn" and "in a hilltown among roses" are as concentrated as any image that can be found in a *tanka*.' Perhaps, then, Hartmann's widely accessible prose as well as his poetry helped to introduce Japanese poetic principles to English-language writers.

Compared to the Japanese masters like Matsuo Bashō and Kobayashi Issa, who wrote thousands of poems each, Hartmann wrote only a few dozen, but he not so modestly reminds us in his introductory remarks to *Japanese Rhythms,* 'one had to write in Old Japan only three or four perfect tanka to be considered a poet'. Furthermore, Hartmann explains to his Western audience that haiku 'was favored in the sixteenth century. Frequently it is purely pictorial and the association of thought produced too vague to be conveyed in English with such exaggerated brevity'. After 100 years of practice, however, English-language writers and readers have become more familiar with the form. We know now that a typical haiku features a word or phrase that signals the season (*kigo*) either in the first or third line; a cutting word (*kireji*) that divides the poem marking the moment when a reader is asked to make an epistemological leap or association; and a theme that connects nature with humanity.

It was Hartmann who explained that haiku ought to create 'a unison of the external beauties of nature and the subtleties of the human soul, which has its origin in tradition and a continual association with flowers, with animals, trees, mountains and the everchanging elements.'[37] And, of course, the brevity of the form itself mirrors the concept of *mono no aware*, a recognition of beauty in its transience.

Consider for example the following haiku by Hartmann:

Oh, red maple leaves,
There seem more of you these eves
    Than ever grew on trees!

The 'red maple leaves' signal autumn, the word 'eves' cuts the poem, and Hartmann's innovative addition of rhyme reinforces the unity of the first two lines. The word 'seem' incorporates human subjectivity. At this late point in autumn, the speaker suddenly realizes a difference between leaves on a tree and leaves strewn on the ground. The nature of that difference is left up to the reader. We need to make a leap. For instance, we might remember the fleeting beauty of the tree on the first day that all of its leaves shifted from green to red, its blazing unity, though we are now surrounded by incontrovertible signs of loss. Most English-language readers in the twenty-first century understand how to appreciate this kind of poetic experience, but it was in the early twentieth that Sadakichi Hartmann began to prepare us.

Even though it has taken us 100 years to begin to acknowledge Hartmann's contributions as a poet, he would have considered himself a success from the start. Among possible titles for an autobiography that he never completed Hartmann included *Success in Failure*. He understood that 'true artists' like himself were not likely to succeed in terms of fortune or fame: 'The true artist … has ever preferred to worship his lofty and often narrow ideals in poverty and obscurity, rather than to waste his genius on the vain world, which has but little in common with his dreams and aspirations.'[38] In particular, he understood his audience's limited taste for poetry: 'With current devaluations, poetry is not on par anywhere. When only material progress is at stake, poetry does not function.'[39] Hence, Hartmann self-published most of his poetry in limited manuscript editions not to make a profit but to share his art with a limited few. In the third person, Hartmann wrote of himself in 1919: 'He has always remained true to his own belief not in art for art's sake or art for humanity's sake, but art by the few and for the few.'[40] Hartmann's ambition with *My Rubaiyat* aimed at chambermaids and businessmen was an exception. For the most part, Hartmann was willing to be recognized as a success 'by the few'. At the end of his life, which he spent in a shack he built near his daughter Wistaria Linton, on the Morongo Indian Reservation in Banning, California, Hartmann continued to create art by painting and writing, and he continued to communicate his ideas about art by lecturing and corresponding.

During his final year, Hartmann composed his own characteristically unconventional obituary, part prose and part poem. In it the speaker describes the sounds of ringing bells and ocean waves that rise in alarm and perturbation as Hartmann's death approaches. At the end, however, these sounds cease, replaced by one more epistemological surprise. Falling flowers make an incredible racket: 'Sadakichi Hartmann is gone a new scene is on / sounds like flowers drop one by one // Bing! Bang! Bung! Bing! Bong! / Bung! Bing! Bing! Bong! Bang!'

Hartmann died in 1944 while visiting his daughter in St Petersburg, Florida, but his poems live on, each one making its own glorious racket.

A NOTE ON THE TEXTS

Like his mentor Walt Whitman, who revised his works multiple times over the course of his life, Sadakichi Hartmann believed that some poems are 'never complete' and might 'undergo many changes'.* In practice, however, Hartmann made relatively few and minor changes to his poems over his long career. For instance, his tanka and haiku, which appeared first in the 1904 'Manuscript Edition' of *Drifting Flowers of the Sea and Other Poems*, saw many additions but few alterations in subsequent editions in 1916, 1920, and 1933 under the title *Japanese Rhythms*. In 1904, Hartmann included only six tanka and no haiku, but in the 1933 handwritten edition, he presented twenty tanka, seventeen haiku, and four dodoitsu. Among the few significant changes that he made over those years was in the last line of 'Tanka VIII'. Earlier he had written 'I may live as butterfly' but later preferred 'I may sport as butterfly'. In this volume, I have decided to reproduce Hartmann's latest choices, taking them to be the imperfect but best indications of his final intentions. However, I have corrected mistakes (e.g., replacing 'adoom' with 'abloom') and added words accidentally left out of lines that otherwise make sense (e.g., 'not' in sentences that require logical negation). In his later work, Hartmann tended to add exclamation points, which seem to signal ecstatic surprise or a simultaneous interjection and interrogation. In general, I have preserved his latest punctuation only sometimes reverting to the punctuation of an earlier version for the sake of clarity. Hartmann occasionally varied his indentations, especially when he was switching from script to typeset editions or

---

* Hartmann, 'Instead of a Preface,' *My Rubaiyat.*

vice versa. In these cases, I have preferred his script indentations in order to give a sense of his style at its freest. To honor Hartmann's paratextual choices I have reproduced his original order of poems within each volume and included dates of composition whenever he did.

During his long career Hartmann attempted many poetic forms with varying degrees of success and longevity. Some of his early poems do not even register as poems to contemporary readers, yet I have included them in this volume to give a sense of what he deemed important in subject and form. Certainly his 'erotic' poems in *Naked Ghosts* might seem tame or even stilted today, but women of his time loved them. The language of 'Cyanongen Seas' still seduces. *Drifting Flowers* mixes poems written after Whitman with a few tanka and 'The Pirate', a narrative poem with musical tempo markings fit only to inspire an early draft of 'Growltiger's Last Stand'. Even though 'To the "Flat Iron"' stands the test of time, in that its speaker imagines a future in which that building would be admired 'Without shame', some of its language looks backwards to the nineteenth century – 'limpid light' and 'madd'ning roar'. Hartmann himself admits the limitations of his third book, *My Rubaiyat*. The last book that he continued to revise and expand was *Japanese Rhythms*. Like Kobayashi Issa before him, Hartmann knew that one way to find rare success was to risk frequent failure.

In his essay 'Why I Publish My Own Books', Hartmann explained that he privileged freedom over profit.[*] Writing about himself in the third person, he insisted that he would 'maintain his independence by hook or crook, no matter how, and publish his efforts as well as he can for those few

---

[*] Hartmann, 'Why I Publish My Own Books,' *Greenwich Village* 3 (Nov. 1915): 15–17.

who can cherish them.' Referring to his use of mimeograph machines and hand copying, Hartmann acknowledged 'the poverty-stricken make-up of my author's editions, so out of place in this modern book world of gilt edges, padding, liberal margins, and embossed covers.' He hoped that one day a conventional publisher would 'command a larger clientele for me – but I am not inclined to go out of my way for one … Having waited so long, I can afford to wait a few years longer.' One hundred and one years after he wrote that essay, Little Island Press ends his wait. This volume reprints all of his poetry books – albeit without gilt edges – as well as some poems that heretofore one could consult only among the Sadakichi Hartmann Papers at the Special Collections of the University of California, Riverside.

In one previously unpublished manuscript, Hartmann's speaker wonders, 'If words of mine / Own strength to live / Centuries hence … ' Some of Sadakichi Hartmann's poems bear traces of trends that ended long ago. Some inspired Modernist poets that exceed him in fame. And some own the strength to live on their own in this new century.

CHRONOLOGY

1867 Carl Sadakichi Hartmann born on
8 November on Dejima Island in the harbor of
Nagasaki, Japan, to Carl Hermann Oskar and
Osada Hartmann

1868 Osada dies; Sadakichi and his older brother,
Taru, sent to be raised by their grandmother
and Uncle Ernst in Hamburg, Germany

1881 Hartmann forced to attend German Imperial
Naval Academy but escapes to Paris

1882 Hartmann sent to be raised by uncle and aunt
in Philadelphia, Pennsylvania; he works as a
spittoon and window cleaner, press feeder,
lithographic stippler, clerk in a tombstone
factory, perfume peddler, and negative
retoucher; he also reads his way through two
libraries and several bookstores

1884 Hartmann visits Walt Whitman in Camden,
New Jersey

1885 With proceeds from selling his personal
library, Hartmann travels in Europe

1887 Hartmann tries and fails to establish the Walt
Whitman Society with himself as its head

1888 Hartmann travels to Belgium, Holland, and
England and meets the Rossettis

1889 Hartmann publishes *Poems*, a collection of work inspired by Whitman and the Symbolists

1889–91 Hartmann writes for *The New York Herald* and *Philadelphia Times*

1891 During a severe bout of depression, Hartmann meets and marries Elizabeth Blanche Walsh; later that year their first child, Dorothea, is born

1892–93 Hartmann writes for Samuel McClure's newspaper syndicate as a roving reporter in Paris, where he meets Mallarmé, Monet, Whistler, Verlaine, Debussy, and Maeterlinck

1893 Hartmann writes for the *Weekly Review*; he establishes *The Art Critic* in Boston and sells 750 subscriptions; he is arrested for publishing his Symbolist play, *Christ*, and spends Christmas week in the Charles Street Jail

1894 Hartmann becomes a naturalized US citizen listing 'Emperor of Germany' as his previous 'nationality'; he exhibits his pastel paintings for the first time

1895 Hartmann publishes *Conversations with Walt Whitman*

1896 Hartmann publishes a realistic play entitled *A Tragedy in a New York Flat;* he writes but does not publish a Symbolist play entitled *Mohammed*

1897   Hartmann's prose-poem 'Leitmotif' serves as the introduction to Ann Throop's *Whisperings of a Wind Harp*; he also edits and publishes *Art News* and a Symbolist play entitled *Buddha*, from which he reads at Bruno's Garrett in Greenwich Village

1898   Hartmann publishes *Naked Ghosts* which includes poems written as early as 1887

1899   Hartmann publishes a collection of short stories under the title *Shopenhauer in the Air* and begins writing for Alfred Stieglitz's journal *Camera Notes*; Ann Throop gives birth to their son, Robert

1898–1902   Hartmann works as a staff writer for the *New Yorker Staats-Zeitung* and publishes some articles on pictorial photography in *The Criterion*

1901   Hartmann publishes *Shakespeare in Art*

1902   Hartmann publishes two-volume *History of American Art* and *Modern American Sculpture*

1903   Edgar is the last child born to Hartmann and Elizabeth; Hartmann publishes an expanded version of *Naked Ghosts*

1904   Hartmann publishes *Drifting Flowers of the Sea and Other Poems* dedicated to Elizabeth Blanche Walsh, *Japanese Art*, and 'The

Japanese Conception of Poetry' in *Reader Magazine*

1906   Hartmann founds *Mother Earth : A Monthly Magazine Devoted to Social Science and Literature* with Emma Goldman and other anarchists

1907   Hartmann meets Lillian Bonham at an artists' colony in Aurora, New York

1908   Hartmann publishes an expanded edition of *Shopenhauer in the Air*

1909   Hartmann publishes *Composition in Portraiture*

1910   Hartmann publishes *My Theory of Soul-Atoms*; he also begins editing and publishing *The Stylus*. His brother, Taru, is living in Denver, Colorado, at this time until at least 1930

1911   Wistaria is the third child born to Hartmann and Lillian Bonham

1913   Hartmann publishes *My Rubaiyat*

1915   Hartmann publishes a chapbook edition of *Tanka and Haikai* and *Permanent Peace : Is It a Dream?*

1916   Hartmann publishes an expanded edition of *My Rubaiyat*; he produces Ibsen's play *Ghosts* in San Francisco

1919   Hartmann publishes *Landscape and Figure Composition* and *The Whistler Book*, which some critics consider to be his best book of art criticism

1920   Hartmann publishes an expanded edition of tanka, haiku, and dodoitsu under the title *Japanese Rhythms*; and a novella entitled *The Last Thirty Days of Christ*

1923   Hartmann publishes a Symbolist play entitled *Confucius* and moves to Southern California; he writes a film script entitled *Don Quixote* but is unable to produce it

1924   Hartmann plays the role of Court Magician in Douglas Fairbanks' *Thief of Bagdad*

1925   Republishes *Naked Ghosts;* he works as the Hollywood correspondent for the British theatre magazine *Curtain*

1926   Hartmann publishes a mimeograph edition of *Japanese Rhythms*; Jonquil is the last child born to Hartmann and Lillian

1927   Publishes *Passport to Immortality*

1931   Publishes *My Crucifixion* about his struggle with asthma

1932   Publishes a revised edition of *History of American Art*

1933   Publishes an expanded limited edition of *Japanese Rhythms*

1934   Hartmann writes a Symbolist play entitled *Moses*

1935   Hartmann completes manuscript for *Esthetic Verities* and donates it to the Ridgeway Library in Philadelphia

1938   Hartmann builds and lives in a shack named 'Catclaw Siding' on land owned by his daughter Wistaria Linton on the Morongo Indian Reservation near Banning, California; he writes but does not publish a play entitled *Baker Eddy*

1940   Hartmann publishes *Strands and Ravelings of the Art Fabric*

1942   President Franklin D. Roosevelt signs executive order 9066 authorizing the internment of Japanese Americans; Hartmann is interviewed by the FBI but avoids being interned; Hartmann begins to compile a volume of collected poems but does not finish

1944   Hartmann dies during a visit with daughter Dorothea Gilliland in St Petersberg, Florida

NAKED GHOSTS (1903)

The Goddess of Love seems a fiery mare before you have the courage to mount her, but turns into a decrepit jade after the first encounter.

OH, MIASMIC SWAMPS OF SOUTHERN CLIMES

Oh, Miasmic swamps of Southern climes
Voluptuous summer nights preceding a
    thunderstorm!
Luxurious sensuality of erotic art and
    literature!
Oh, half veiled limbs of modern Circes!
Untraceable exhalations of half decent
    loves
Hypocritical, bestial, deep eyed morbidities
    of modern civilization lulling our senses
    to a lethean sleep for which there is no
    dawn.
Even you do not exist in vain, also you are
    notes of the immortal hymn of love
    which sounds in every human breast!

(1887)

OH, TO CREATE!!

Oh, to Create. All to create whoever they may be!
Whoever works with hand or brain helps progress to
   advance!
Oh, to fill a position which enables me to show good will
   and love to every one!
To be an artist, to throw one's whole existence into the
   work which shall reveal the mystery of a soul to man!

Oh, to be a poet to write with feverish haste, the hand
   scarce apt to hold the pen: words, idea for
   ages to come!

To be a prominent man to make with one word millions of
   people satisfied!

Still nobler the divine joy of a man embracing the woman
   he loves!

Greatest of all to be a mother in child-bed laboring under
   the heaviest pains! What serene feelings are
   pressed with the child to life! What bliss
   does rouse her in nursing her new born babe,
   warm with the warmth of her body.

Oh, men and women, this one word *create* links all of us
   to one chain of harmony, for everyone owes the
   expression of this sublime idea, and every voice
   joins in my enthusiastic cry: *Oh, to create!*

(1887)

AT LAST THE NUPTIAL NIGHT OF
TWO CHASTE LOVERS

It is midnight, they are alone and nothing existing to separate them. For years and years their
souls have been one and now for the first time,
their bodies shall be united as close as love and
love can do.

There they lie, breast to breast, enraptured with
delight and happiness. And so they rest united
while the fluids of life and love are flowing
and flowing and mingling with each other. That
is sensuality! But a sensuality so sublime, that
it almost touches heaven!

And now the first hours of night are passed and
with glowing cheeks and smiling faces, husband and
wife sleep quietly hand in hand! Friends, meditate!
This is more philosophic than you think! Sleep on,
sleep on, happy ones, and yon gentle winds of night
warble their redolent joys from land to land and
whisper into their ears of young or old: At last the
Nuptial Night of two chaste lovers.

(1887)

SIGNS OF VIRGINITY

To Various Ladies

Quaint shadows are silently floating athwart the
    Lethean well – dim crimson lamps illumine
    the wilds of asphodel.

The river of night is flowing through the rills
    of the midland vale – breakers at distant
    seashores rear in the fury of the gale.

And unloved limbs like branches tossing in
    dismal rain, while the thirsty soul sips
    ecstasy from every drop of pain.

(1889)

CONTRAST

The dissonance of misery and wealth in dreamy
reverie floats as long as the heart and the brain are young.

But when hymns of admiration obscure the days
of hope, then dreams among books, and books among
dreams can keep no longer the lamp alight.

And opening roses in wild embrace sink love
faint to the ground, and silver laughs ring through
the night, through the deluge of light and chime
with desire, warm bodies and thought.

While wings of fame, white and ghostlike, are
fluttering in twilight's realm, and love under
vibrations dissolves in musical rhyme, a flaring
of carmine kisses the raven locks of youth, and
streams in flowerless cadence to the silent seas
of truth.

A golden aurora for countless years is rising
from lonesome graves, while laurel crowns lie broken
on marble steps and biers.

(1889)

MAIDEN, I KNOW THE SORROW

Maiden, I know the sorrow that haunts thee
with sleepless nights, when thy midnight life is
illumined with imagination's vagrom lights.

Thy gentle dream of desire woos a flower
among the dead, Lord Byron, thy phantom lover,
strews roses, red with fire, upon thy lonesome bed.

And rain pearls dim with passion anoint thy
throbbing breast, thy virgin dream of beauty sounds
the song of danaidel unrest.

(1892)

A STORY OFTEN TOLD

They wandered homeward one summer night,
The air was sultry, and the moon shone bright.

The following morning her eyes were red;
He had left the village, for her he was dead.

Scarce nine months after she had killed her child.
Him the law was hunting through swamp and wild.

The parents received with the latest mail;
That he – at the gallows, and she – in jail.

Yet at the place of their first sweet kiss
The violets grew as if nothing amiss.

(1887)

HOURS OF MIDNIGHT

I

The fires of the day have vanished in the
magic flames of night, and half of mankind
lies dreaming in calm and subdued light.

The lines of passion are glowing in the
mysterious book of life, and luscious songs
are flowing through the realms of connubial
strife.

Maternity's light is rising from the dawn-
seas of the earth, the spawn (essence) of future
generations is rolling through the starlit universe.
    (spinning)

II

A chaos of love is surging in the purple depth
of shame, as the languid chalice opens beneath
love's satanic flame.

Vistas of paradise are uncovered in every fiery
kiss; the demons of creation are hissing in
every sigh of bliss.

Pale rivers of pain are bursting form the
saturnalian fountain of lust, and the chalice
of love is deluged in succulent disgust.

III

Two bodies lie united in delirious joy and pain
while the bridal chamber is resounding with
love's mysterious strain.

The gates of virginity are yielding to the nervous
longing of youth, the halls of womanhood are
widening with nature's sublime truth.

The road of creation lies open to the vandals of
the soul, the temple of the body looms at eternity's
pole.

IV

The sacred hours are haunted by disenchantments'
feverish glow, the source of love is dying, the
waters of life sink low.

The woods grow wan and discolored in enervation's
fanatic rites, the branches of spring sway moaning
in dull and dismal nights.

The wayworn wanderers of love lie prostrate near
the goal, the monotonous labor of lust exterminates
(chills) body and soul.

(1890)

POEMS TO EVA

I

Rose of love, be not ashamed of thy languid
grace, of thy trembling nakedness in the
sun's embrace.

For the kiss of ardent suns is thy life's
desire and the flood of golden light feeds
thy wanton soul of fire.

And the dewdrops trembling in the dusky
lowland grass are the pearls thy soul is
weeping, as the reapers pass.

II

Tonight I feel so weary, I long for an hour
of rest, an hour where I may lie dreaming
on the ivory of your breast.

An hour of innocent longing, when even our
lips do not meet, when only the dreams of
our souls in silence each other greet.

An hour of dreaming sadness among the sounds
and gleams of night, an hour of secret yearning
for dawn and radiant light.

III

And if in hours of midnight, you long for
my fierce embrace, give vent to those lambent
feelings that flush your body and face.

Dream that your limbs are encircling the furious
passions of night, that your quivering soul is
sounding vast symphonies of light.

IV

The dawn of your life was illusive, though its
colors were iridescent and bright, the flower
fields of your body longed for the rains of night.

The torches of love extinguished in sad and
silent gloom, the poppy's red petals have
withered in the midst of their virginal bloom.

New darkness is hovering around you, your body
and soul are in strife, but through the clouds
of passion shines the star of a woman's life.

(1890–91)

A STRAIN IN RED

An eager tongue between parted lips, a garnet
glow within argent hips, the blood of roses
whose thorns pierce my heart, as I sip love's
wine over the senescent embers of art, where
ruffians scoff the hierophant's robe in fire
sunsets of dying globes.

(1882)

THE COURTESAN'S COMPLAINT

When within me you move like a dream,
your soul roam o'er distant streams, on
whose surface idoneously gleam strange
flowers of other lives.

For love is destined to doom, when passion
in starlit gloom spins in her sinister
loom the shroud for the joys of night.

(1897)

WHITE LADY OF MY DESIRES

Sleep on and smile thy radiant smile amid
dawn-flowers, frail and white, while naked
ghosts kiss thy body's soul as they pass in
their magic flight, and I stand lone and
shivering in the white and withering night.

(1892)

MYSTERIOUS FLIRTATION

The night of dreams is over, the day is sick
with rain, the melody of the body has a sad
and dark refrain.

The snow of roses lies scattered like raiments
of lust and shame, the gold of the soul is
melting in passion's lambent flame.

Again the body is glowing under lilies of
fragrant white, and civilization whirling in
dances wild and bright.

Again lightnings of violence are flashing from
mountain to mountain of lust, as the eagle of
love is cleaving the clouds of amorous dust.

(1889)

MELODY IN BLACK AND WHITE

Gertrude, as white as marble with hair as
black as night, unclasps her silver girdle
that sparkles in the darkness of light.

Knight Death, who is her suitor, casts
aside his mantle of gloom, and his ghostly
form dances rattling in the white rays of
the moon.

She rends her robe to lure him to the ebon
depth of her shame, but the naked knight
desires no light from the darkness of his
dame.

He squats upon the inky ground, and claws
a deep hole with his clattering bones till
the grave grows deep, till the grave grows
wide to the music of her groans.

He drags her down to the nuptial bed, wrapt
tight in her mantle of raven hair, and
darkness embraces her sinful life under
the moonlight's laughing glare.

(1892)

THE WANTON ROSE

A rose is opening her chalice with the
charm of a wanton's art, and offers her
languid beauty for sale on passion's mart.

The bee is the highest bidder in love
with her purple hue, and scattering gold he
revels in her lap of redolent dew.

In vain for her falling garments the queenly
maiden gropes, the golden shrine bursts open
with the jewelled seed of secret hopes.

(1891)

PROSTITUTE FLOWERS
(from *Christ*, Act III)

When gardens lie dreaming in moonlight,
the nocturnal flower begins her reign,
unfastening her mantle of glimmering white,
perfuming the air with a sinful strain.

The night moths are lured to the dangerous
fire, each sips the nectar of her desire,
while her soul is yearning for unknown
treasures that can never be hers in her
life of pleasures.

(1891)

BROKEN LILY

Last evening as I passed through the meadows
a lily greeted my sight. I had not the heart
to break her though I longed for a wanton
night.

This morning I found her broken in tears
o'er incontinence wept, while silently through
the meadows the sighs of her fragrance swept.

And strange, I envied the hand by which she
was slain, while for her broken fragrance I
felt but a passing pain.

(1892)

IN DECIDUOUS HOURS OF FIERCE UNREST

In deciduous hours of fierce unrest, bound,
Dolorosa, unto my breast, with life's blood
incarnadine my pallid lips and encircle my
loins with thy loveladen hips!

Drown, Dolorossa, thy silent lust in the ebb
and tide of evacuent bliss, and halo the
dawn of thy life's desire with the love–
bedewed flames of maternity's fire!

(1895)

CYANOGEN SEAS ARE SURGING

Cyanogen seas are surging over fierce
cinnabarine strands, where white amazons
are marching in the radiance of the sands.

Oh, were my lambent love flame but like
the surging sea, deluge the red of the
desert and drown the white virgins in me.

(1897)

DRIFTING FLOWERS OF THE SEA
AND OTHER POEMS (1904)

To Elizabeth Blanche Walsh

You remember the good monk who was returning to the convent and, as he rested by the wayside beneath an oak tree, listening to the nightingale's song, fell fast asleep.

When he woke the sun was low. He stood up shivering and asked an old peasant who was passing what time it was.

'Seven o'clock,' said the peasant.

'Oh, oh, then I shall not reach the monastery before nightfall.'

'What monastery?' asked the surprised peasant.

'The monastery of St. Withold, two leagues from here.'

'So, ho', said the peasant, 'you are one of those odd antiquary people, too. I thought so when I saw your odd clothes. But you are taking a useless journey – there is nothing to see, except some old stones at the gates.'

'Sacked!' cried the monk, 'demolished since morning –'

'Oh, long ago,' said the peasant, 'the father of my grandfather saw it standing – it was a hundred years ago. Since then it has been a ruin.'

The good monk had slept a hundred years listening to the nightingale's song.

When I laid aside Sadakichi Hartmann's colorful pages and came down into the market place, where the books of the day are cried, I feel as composed and exceptional as the good monk of St. Withold.

And yet –

Vance Thompson

NOCTURNE

Upon the silent sea-swept land
  The dreams of night fall soft and gray
    The waves fade on the jeweled sand
      Like some lost hope of yesterday.

The dreams of night fall soft and gray
  Upon the summer-colored seas,
    Like some lost hope of yesterday,
      The sea-mew's song is on the breeze.

Upon the summer-colored seas
  Sails gleam and glimmer ghostly white,
    The sea-mew's song is on the breeze
      Lost in the monotone of night.

Sails gleam and glimmer ghostly white,
  They come and slowly drift away,
    Lost in the monotone of night,
      Like visions of a summer-day.

They shift and slowly drift away
  Like lovers' lays that wax and wane,
    The visions of a summer-day
      Whose dreams we ne'er will dream again.

Like lovers' lays wax and wane
  The star dawn shifts from sail to sail,
    Like dreams we ne'er will dream again;
      The sea-mews follow on their trail.

The star dawn shifts from sail to sail,
  As they drift to the dim unknown,
    The sea-mews follow on their trail
      In quest of some dreamland zone.

In quest of some far dreamland zone,
  Of some far silent sea-swept land,
    They are lost in the dim unknown,
      Where waves fade on jewelled sand
        And dreams of night fall soft and gray,
          Like some lost hope of yesterday.

RECEDING TIDE

Faint and languid falls the twilight,
  Murmuring its mystic runes,
    Waves recede from drowsy shorelands,
     Ghostly pale, in whispering tunes,
      Reeds are gently blowing seawards –
       Wind and night are on the dunes!

Reeds are gently blowing seawards,
  While the mournsome autumn breeze,
    Wandering over drowsy shorelands,
     Dances roundelays in trees,
      And the waters, hurrying leewards,
       Never in their revels cease.

Ghostly pale, in whispering tunes,
  From the duneland wild and gray,
    Wreathed with stars and flowers of foam,
     Restless to the East they stray,
      With the mournful autumn breeze
       To some star-isle far away.

Receding till lost in the darkness
  Like twilight's languid song,
    Like flowers of fire and stars of foam
     That to nocturnal seas belong,
      Like life and love with their mystic runes
       When night and wind are on the dunes.

WHY I LOVE THEE?

Why I love thee?
Ask why the seawind wanders,
Why the shore is aflush with the tide,
Why the moon through heaven meanders
Like seafaring ships that ride
On a sullen, motionless deep;
Why the seabirds are fluttering the strand
Where the waves sing themselves to sleep
And starshine lives in the curves of the sand!

WHY I NO LONGER LOVE THEE?

Why I no longer love thee?
　Ask why summer has fled,
Why autumn is dead with its garnet glow,
Why the sea is gray and the sky is gray;
　Why bitter gales o'er the salt flats blow,
　Where the sea-fowl sport in ghoulish play
And the pods of the beach-pea stand withered
On the long-curved rifts of dream-torn sand;
　Why the shore is scarred by time's rough hand,
　　And ships that heel on wintry seas
　　　Are wrecked on the ashen strand!

DRIFTING FLOWERS OF THE SEA

Across the dunes, in the waning light,
The rising moon pours her amber rays,
Through the slumberous air of the dim, brown night
The pungent smell of seaweed strays –
  From vast and trackless spaces
    Where wind and water meet,
      White flowers, that rise from the sleepless deep,
        Come drifting to my feet.
  They flutter the shore in a drowsy tune,
    Unfurl their bloom to the lightlorn sky,
      Allow a caress to the rising moon,
        Then fall to slumber, and fade, and die.

White flowers, a-bloom on the vagrant deep,
Like dreams of love rising out of sleep,
You are the songs I dreamt but never sung,
Pale hopes my thoughts alone have known,
Vain words ne'er uttered, though on the tongue,
That winds to the sibilant seas have blown.
  In you, I see the everlasting drift of years
    That will endure all sorrows, smiles and tears;
      For when the bell of time will ring the doom
        To all the follies of the human race,
          You still will rise in fugitive bloom
            And garland the shores of ruined space.

IMMACULATE CONCEPTION

A maiden flower stands lonesome on a vast and
  desolate plain, in trembling fear that
  her longings for life and love prove vain.

But the passing breeze takes pity, it embraces
  some flowering plant and carries its golden
  riches to the bride of the desolate land.

Windstirred she tosses her clustering hair to the
  dust of golden glow, and flower-starred with
  the waxing morn the desolate meadows grow.

A TRIOLET

'Tis the first day of spring!
The catkins are a-bloom,
The bluebirds are a-wing,
'Tis the first day of spring!

Faint scents the breezes bring;
Man's thoughts new shape assume.
'Tis the first day of spring,
The catkins are a-bloom!

PARFUM DES FLEURS

Oh, frail and fragrant visions,
　Sweet nomads of the air,
　　That rise like the mist on the meadows
　　　And cling to my darksome hair,

Are ye the souls of roses,
　Of memory's vagrom lays,
　　Sent to caress my senses –
　　　Faint murmurs of bygone days?

TWILIGHT HOURS

I

The colors of the rainbow are fading in the silent
    and distant West, and the heartache of
    twilight trembles within my aching breast.

  For the light of my love has faded like sunbeams
    in the West, and the color of twilight will
    tremble forever in my breast.

II

I think of thy kindness often, when lonesome I feel
    and cold, I have not forgotten our childhood,
    nor your loving words of old.

  And still my sweetest songs of life are floating
    in dreams to thee, like whisperings at eventide,
    across a clouded sea.

III

We two are sitting in the bark, and listen to the
    wavelets' play, the shore is melting in the
    dark, day's echoes silently decay.

  Oh life, with all thy hopes so fair, wilt thou
    too float away, like visions rising in the
    air that greet the parting day!

IV

She stands amidst the roses, and tears dart from her
    eye that like the fragrant roses her soul
      must fade and die.

  He stares at the twilight ocean on the shore of a
     foreign land, a faded rose is trembling
       within his soft white hand.

V

The rushes whisper softly, the sounds of silence wake,
    large flowers like sad remembrance float
      on the dark green lake.

  Were life but like the waters, so bright and calm
     and deep, and love like floating flowers
       that on the surface meet.

VI

The naked trees of autumn grope shivering through
    twilight's gloom, athwart the whispering branches
      its dying embers loom.

  I dream of life's defoliation, as I watch with
     silent dread, leaf after leaf departing, like
       hopes long withered and dead.

VII

In haunting hours of twilight dreams restless the
    turbulent sea, and heaves her white wanton
    bosom in endless mystery.

  Dream on, dream on, titanic queen, beloved sea, at
     thy wanton breast, I would find rest
     in endless mystery.

[Tanka I–VI originally included here came to appear in
Japanese Rhythms]

DAWN-FLOWERS

To Maurice Maeterlinck

Weird phantoms rise in the dawn-wind's blow,
    In the land of shadows the dawn-flowers grow;
        The night-worn moon yields her weary glow
            To the morn-rays that over the dream-waste flow.

Oh, to know what the dawn-wind murmurs
    In the chapels of pines to the ashen moons;
What the forest-well whispers to dale and dell
    With her singular, reticent runes;
To know the plaint of each falling leaf
    As it whirls across the autumnal plain;
To know the dreams of the desolate shore
    As sails, like ghosts, pass o'er the dawnlit main!
        To know, oh, to know
    Why all life's strains have the same refrain
            As of rain,
        Beating sadly against thy window pane.

    We do not know and we can not know,
    And all that is left for us here below
    (Since 'songs and singers are out of date'
    And the muses have met with a similar fate)
        Is to flee to the land of shadows and dreams,
            Where the dawn-flowers grow
            And dawn-winds blow,
        As morn-rays over life's dream-waste flow
            To drown the moon in their ambient glow.

ENVOY [DAWN-FLOWERS]

Oh, gray dawn-poet of Flanders,
   Though in this life we ne'er may meet,
      I'll linger where thy dream-maids wander
         To strew these dawn-flowers at their feet.

TO THE 'FLAT IRON'

On roof and street, on park and pier,
The springtide sun shines soft and white,
Where the 'Flat Iron', gaunt, austere,
Lifts its huge tiers in limpid light.

From the city's stir and madd'ning roar
Your monstrous shape soars in massive flight,
And 'mid the breezes the ocean bore
Your windows flame in the sunset light.

Lonely and lithe, o'er the nocturnal city's
Flickering flames, you proudly tower,
Like some ancient, giant monolith,
Girt with the stars and mists that lower.

All else we see fade fast and disappear,
Only your prow-like form looms gaunt, austere,
As in a sea of fog, now veiled, now clear.

Iron structure of the time,
Rich, in showing no pretense,
Fair, in frugalness sublime,
Emblem staunch of common sense,
Well may you smile over Gotham's vast domain,
As dawn greets your pillars with roseate flame,
For future ages will proclaim
Your beauty, boldly,
Without shame.

AS THE LINDENS SHIVER IN AUTUMN DREAMS

The fields lie wrapt in autumn dreams,
  Beneath the dim, blue vault of night,
    The moon, like a bark on sluggish streams,
      Spreads soft her sail of silver light.

Beneath the blue, dim vault of night,
  With the way-worn notes of joy and care,
    Across the sea of the moon's pale light
      Dark flocks of birds flap the silent air.

With the way-worn notes of joy and care
  Fantastic shapes with wings outspread,
    Dark flocks of birds flap the silent air,
      Like a cloud of ominous dread.

Fantastic shapes with wings outspread,
  Droning some harsh and ghoulish tune,
    Like a cloud of ominous dread,
      They darken the sail of the white full moon.

They darken the sail of the soft white moon,
  Like pageants of some Valpurgis night,
    Droning some harsh and ghoulish tune,
      Their rustling wings are shimmering bright.

Their rustling wings are shimmering bright
  As in myriad swarms they are passing by,
    Like pageants of some Valpurgis night,
      Wheeling their flight to some summer sky.

Wheeling their flight whence summer has flown,
  Like dreams and hopes now long gone by,
    Like songs of love our youth has known,
      In myriad swarms they sail the sky.

Like clouds a-sail on glassy streams —
  Gray memories of autumn dreams;
    Like visions of love forever flown,
      You, aerial voyagers, wing your flight
        To some enchanted realm our youth has known,
          Beneath the dim, blue vault of night.

LOVE BY THE SEA

Far away from the murmuring town,
  In the region of sand and sea,
    Love has surprised us on the down –
      Love has surprised you and me –
        In this realm where sea-kissed grasses sway,
          Where winds at nightfall sadly moan,
            Where sea-gulls sing their plaintive lay,
              And waves croon in minor monotone.

No flower grows in this land of dreams,
  No human habitation far or near
    Illumines the scene with a reddish gleam,
      All around is desolate and drear;
        Nothing but weeds and grayish sand –
          Yet the sea seems to say in an undertone;
            Until dawn whitens this wind-blown strand,
              The treasures of night are all thy own!

And like waves that softly shoreward creep,
  Love draws us nigh as the hours pass,
    Thy fluttering hair around me sweep,
      Thy breath is like wind in the weft of the grass;
        I feel thy bosom ebb and tide –
          Its paleness resembles the moonlit sea –
            And as sea and heaven together glide
              Let thy sweetness be lost in me.

Do not be startled at the seabird's cry
  Nor at the wind's relentless blast,
    Too soon the kiss on our lips will die,
      Alas, the joys of Venus never last!
        Like flowers that droop on the sunburnt sward
          Our love must needs wither and fade,
            Like blossoms that are carried seawards
              By the wind from some sleepy glade.

The joys of Venus never last,
  Love is naught but some dreamland lore,
    And as the hours are ebbing fast
      Our dream, like seaweed, will be left on the shore;
        Already the cup of the autumn moon
          Floods with her gold the distant West,
            The bitterness of life will dawn too soon,
              Forlorn lies the sea-gull's last year's nest.

      Perchance, some other autumn eve,
      May greet us on this barren wold,
      Not arm in arm, alone and fain,
      Desirous of the days of old.

The waves have lost their silvery note,
  White birds of dreams o'er the dim plain start,
    Through the mist is gliding a phantom bark –
      What made love open its eyes and part!

Where are the sweet names we whispered low,
  Were they carried away by the breeze?
    The vain words which from our lips did flow
      Are they buried forever in dismal seas?
        And the kisses that rained on your face
          Has nothing remained of their ardent glow?
            The night holds nothing but a cold embrace,
            The sun of our love sank low.

Only the note of the seabird rings
  Through the dim realm of night and mist,
    Not a breath of our past love clings
      To this sea of faded amethyst.
        Even the wind pauses in space
          And refuses to caress our lips;
            Alas, our love was of fleeting pace
            Like the visions of seafaring ships.

Like the flash of a meteor's flight, –
  Know we whither its glow has flown;
    It sped across heaven with radiant light
      And vanished in worlds unknown –
        So the sweet hours have passed away
          Like flowers that on the sand-dunes grow,
            Like waves that die in a wreath of spray
              When bitter winds over the shoreland blow.

SWEET ARE THE DREAMS ON THE BREEZE-BLOWN STRAND
(Sestine Enchainée)

When autumn cloudlets fleck the *sky*
   Straying southward like birds o'er the sea,
      When the flickering sunlight on the dunes
         Is pale, as seagrasses kissed by the spray,
            Seagrasses that knew the summer of yesterday –
               Sweet are the dreams on the breeze-blown strand!

Sweet are the dreams on the breeze-blown strand!
   When cloud skiffs skim athwart the *sky*
      And like a phantom of yesterday
         The light house shimmers out to sea
            Pale as the sand and sea-worn spray
               And the straggling sunlight on the dunes.

Like the straggling sunlight on the dunes,
   Like opal surges that wash the strand
      With briny fragrance, abloom with the spray,
         Like wander-birds that career the *sky*,
            To flowerlit isles of some Southern sea –
               Such are the dreams of yesterday!

Alas, our dreams of yesterday,
   Frail as the fragrance of the dunes,
      Vain as dark jewels of the sea
         Cast up on some glimmering strand,
            They vanish like cloud sails on the *sky*,
               Pale as seagrasses frowsed by the spray.

Pale as seagrasses kissed by the spray,
　Is all this life of yesterday,
　　All our longings for clear blue *skies*
　　　For the low cool plash on autumn dunes,
　　　　All our musings on tide-left strands
　　　　　While birds wing southward o'er the sea.

Like birds winging southward o'er the sea
　Scattered in air-like wasteful spray,
　　Sea-fancies fading on lonesome strands
　　　Weary of storm drifts of yesterday,
　　　　Thus our thoughts on the sea-scooped dunes
　　　　　When autumn cloudlets fleck the *sky*.

Oh, autumn-sea under a cloud-flecked *sky*
　As caressed are thy dunes with opal spray
　　So shimmer in dreams on the breeze-blown strand
　　　Sweet long-lost summers of yesterday.

THE PIRATE

I

Andante con grazia e molto maestoso

The morning dawns, and shakes the stars
   From the raven locks of the queen of night,
     Some ripple down into the sea,
       Some drown in the morning light.

The morning dawns, and strange white forms
   O'er the silent waters stray,
     As if they were searching for falling stars,
      Whose gold has dripped astray,
        Slipped away
      From the rose of morn
       To the shoreless waste,
         That, dull and gray, with its misty bars,
          Yields no reflection to the death of stars.

The morning dawns, and the starting breeze,
   Rends the curtain of silence and mist
     Whence, tinged with roseate morn,
      The pirate's galleon drifts –
       Away from the shore,
      Where the watchfires gleam
      And the sea-gulls scream,
       To her daily toil,
        In quest of spoil
         To waylay some wanderer of the sea.

With plumage strange and wings outspread,
  Like some huge bird from earth long fled,
    The highwayman of the main
        Veers his way
To some blood-red day,
  Out of the silent, gray and shoreless night,
    As the stars ripple down into the sea
      Or drown in the morning light.

II

Allegro con passione

The sea is white with the noonday glare,
  Save a dark unrest and reddish flare
    That troubles the seashine in the West.

There the fight is on —
  With yards entangled and sails aflame,
    Enveloped in clouds that darken the sky,
      Two dark hulls lashed fast together,
        Motionless on the noonday waters lie.

        The fight is on —
Amidst clank of weapons, and powder scent,
  The rattle of muskets, wild shuffle of feet,
    Like the hissing groans of some soul accursed,
      With lightning flares and fanlike bursts,
        Pass shot and shell.

The mouths of the cannons grow a grinning stare,
  With blood are daubed masts and spars,
    And the sparks blown to the lurid air
      Fall on the sails like a rain of stars.

The fight is on –
Black death with his wings of flame
  Now dominates this scene,
    This scene of black and red.
      Like a snake of fire in dismal desire
        He coils up the rigging, chars every plank
          And gnaws his way towards the powder tank,
            While lurid streams of red
              Gush from the wounded and dead
              To the passionless flood,
                Stained with fire and blood.

The hours pass, and the crews are thinned,
  Both demand quarter – but none will strike,
    And still they fight – and fight – and fight –
      Till the blackened masts crash on the burning decks,
        Strewn with bodies in formless stacks.
          The shrieks of the wounded die away,
            Silence takes the place of carnage and fray,
              And as a change to all things must come –
              Even death ceases his fire-song.

Riddled from bow to stern with leaks on the gain
The hulls sink deeper into the passionless main,
Still lashed together as in the hours of fight,
  Like wounded beasts in wild despair,
    They suddenly leap into the lurid air,
      Then roll to the side.
      And glide from day's waning light
        Down to the dismal night
          Of the passionless flood,
            Stained with fire and blood.

The sun swings from the hovering murk,
  Dark crows, that follow the pirate's wake,
    Flap over the crushed timbers and shivered beams,
      Adrift on the blood-stained flood like dismal dreams.

III

Adagio non lamentoso

Thirty times the cannons roar
  Over the black and barren shore
        Of the pirate isle,
      Under whose rifts of shifting sand
        Lies buried the gold, the pirate's hand
          Wrest from the sea wanderer of many a land.

On the black banner that never was furled
  Lies dead the pride of the pirate's race,
    The crew shifts over the quarter deck
      Once more to gaze at his stern sea face.

        Then the anchor is hoisted! –
          Drenched in the twilight's gold
The ship shakes out every sail
            And sweeps before the gales
              Towards the highway of the deep,
              To put its hero forever to sleep.

What mean now thy hoards of gold
  A-dream in the depth of the wind blown sand?
    What remains of thy sea face fantastic and bold
      When you have reached that coral strand,
        Where the mermaids dwell,
          Who love their pirate sweethearts well?

A last farewell to the sun and air,
To the twilight flare
With its pennant unfold
Of crimson and gold!
As strapped to the plank
On the gangway you stand,
To make the bold leap
To the emerald deep.

Harsh as the winds over your life have blown,
Your fate will be in the lands unknown
Of the moonstone twilights of the sea,
And as its currents toss thee from shore to shore
Through coral halls on the moss-grown floor,
Moss-grown since the days of yore,
You still will be,
Fearless and free,
Lord of the sea.

IV

Finale sotto voce e legato

On emerald waves o'er which the moonbeams flow,
Lost like a song on the winds that blow,
An enchanted castle, a phantom sail –
In silent flight from the rolling orb
Pursuing the wanderers of the night –
Strays with the wayward breeze
To be lost on the murmuring seas,

Like a ghost that rose from some emerald tomb
To haunt the murmuring main
And tell the tale of the pirate's doom,
The end of the seaking's reign.

From reddened wave and blackened shore
   The galleon has vanished forever more
     In the moonstone twilights of the sea;
       And only the music the seaweed brings
         Tells of the dauntless deeds of the dead seakings.

MY RUBAIYAT (1916)

To Dunbar Wright, a traveller among Men, who 'in his own way courts the sun and fashions Arcadia of passing winds and flying clouds.'

INSTEAD OF A PREFACE

William Marion Reddy,
  St. Louis Mirror

I will drop the mask and tell you the secret of my verses. You say they impress you as being uneven and unfinished. I heartily agree with you. As I have stated in my announcement to the public, a poem of the scope and range as *My Rubaiyat* is never complete. No doubt, it will undergo many changes within the next ten years. I say ten years deliberately. You see, I possess the arrogance of conviction. I believe it will survive, simply because it strikes a popular chord, and attempts, no matter how vaguely, to reproduce the broken melody that hums in every mind. Somebody else may venture forth on similar paths and succeed to please even the fastidious in rhyme. *My Rubaiyat* may be put on the back shelves. Well, we will see. I look at my work with objective eyes. It is a mere youngster now. It will grow and nobody will watch its growth with keener appreciation than myself. The number of verses will not increase, but I sincerely hope they will gain in clarity and strength as well as in musical and pictorial wealth of expression.

As for versification, let me make this explanation. I chose the eight syllable stanza on account of its terseness of expression. It is least pliable to any rush and swing of rhythm, but most conducive to the conveyance of fragmentary moods and thoughts. The omission of rhyme I essayed for no other reason than its technical difficulty. To make rhymeless lines read like a poem is the most laborious task a songmith can set himself. It is the vanity of the alien to show his mastery over a language that was neither his father's nor his mother's tongue. But I object to your statement that I disdain rhyme. My meter is rough and wilful and subject to impurities, as for instance counting the last two syllables in words like 'happier' and 'sunnier' either as one or two, just as my fancy, or rather my appreciation of rhythm, dictates. My rhythm changes constantly but it is palpable, underneath as it were, at all times. I have some experience as a reader (though elocutionists may shrug their shoulders at my style of interpretation – let them shrug) and I have, whenever I write, the habit of reading aloud the words as I put them down. Reading means to get a certain sense and swing, color and sound in the words as one utters them. If my verses contain this possibility of aural gratification they cannot be utterly devoid of rhythm. No doubt my sense of sound alliteration is foreign, unconsciously Oriental. I feel a sound relation, no, even a rhyme suggestion in words like 'chance' and 'spring', 'herd' and 'feet' at the end of succeeding stanzas. The alliteration of Japanese poets is much subtler (due to the peculiarities of the language) than the word music of our Laniers and Whitmans, although it is never conducted with the elaborate precision of a Poe or Swinburne. It always remains fragmentary, it rarely resembles full orchestration. Also my lines lack the merit of contrapuntal structure. Yet they have one quality which is generally overlooked. They possess pictorial harmony. My long and persistent association with art makes me not only see but think things in pictures. Pictures abound throughout *My Rubaiyat* for all who have the mental pictorial vision to see them. Lines like 'turn phantoms with the colder morn' and 'in a hilltown among roses' are as concentrated as any image that can be found in a *tanka* (i.e. a Japanese short poem).

Critics may contend that pictorial suggestion *per se*, as the main characteristic of a poem, does not conform to the accepted form of poetry. This objection is meaningless to me. Without the spirit of innovation there would have been no incentive to write the poem. Like the composers of the day I believe not in the old ideals but in new methods of expression.

My ambition was to write a simple poem which would appeal to all: to chambermaids as well as cognoscenti, ordinary business men as well as solitary artistic souls. Who will decide whether I have succeeded or failed? Only the public at large. The poem, no doubt, is too didactic for fragile aesthetes who glorify naught but evanescent words, but it is surely no shortcoming to try to express thought. Even exponents of the modern schools attempt this – occasionally. The way of expression is a different matter. It is open to criticism. But excuses that a critic knows nothing about a certain subject, and yet at the same time deliberately pricks at this very thorn in the flesh of his ignorance, are sad to contemplate. Rhyme is surely not out of date. And the supposed lack of rhythm is merely imaginary. Would you enjoy Japanese or Chinese music? Very likely not and yet they contain as fine a rhythm and as musical a quality as any modern composition. Only they are vaguer, subtle, different.

And on this difference hinges all logical and evasive argument. The practical philosophy contained in *My Rubaiyat*, of course, can be attacked for being non-moral or non-religious, but the technique of the poem can be discussed only from one viewpoint.

Sincerely yours,
Sadakichi Hartmann

MY RUBAIYAT

I

What should we dream, what should we say,
On this drear day, in this sad clime!
In the garden the asters fade,
Smoke of weed-fires blurs the plain,
The hours pass with a sullen grace –
Can we be gay when skies are gray!

II

Would joy prove a more steady guest,
In palm-girt, sunnier Southern lands,
Some lambent world of green and gold
Fanned by the charm of Orient lay!
'Tis vain delusion thus to think
That life will change with change of scene.

III

Man cannot get away from facts –
Alas, stern duty looms supreme,
For certain things we must perform,
Obey the inward voices' call.
Calm joyous days cannot be wooed
Unless our conscience is at peace.

IV

Life is to most a weary task,
A ceaseless strife for daily bread,
We cannot act as we would like,
We cannot gain for what we strive.
To bear the burden cheerfully
Is all this earth allows to us.

V

Our tired soul with faint forced smile
But rarely scales the loftier themes,
Fair Hafiz and Anacreon
Have they drunk, laughed and sung in vain!
Do grove and grange no longer yield
The idylls of Theocritus!

VI

Was man once happier than now?
Who is there to tell the story
Of slaves or Caesars of the past?
Still our blood is stirred each spring,
Still our books and music make us dream,
Why mourn the 'snows of yesteryear?'

VII

There were ever some more favored
Who care-free basked in fortune's sun.
The rest did toil. And you and I?
We hear the same recurrent rhymes,
Like changing seasons, night and day,
We simply come, sojourn, and go.

VIII

We enter the world unbidden,
Plod along roads as we know best.
One is born rich, the other poor,
Who knows what helps a mortal most.
Ere sleep we rub from our eyes
We are forever what we are.

IX

The laughter of childhood is gone,
The toy castles we built are lost –
Can we redeem in future days
The disappointments of the past!
Our nursery songs will they change
Into jubilant songs of love!

X

Light-headed youth, all smiles around
In dew-drenched gardens of spring morns
No heed takes of the dial's stealth.
Youth wants to conquer – rule the spheres,
While the sun runs his ruthless course
And shadows begin to lengthen.

XI

In open woods some summer night,
The sound of the wind in the leaves –
Two vagrant lovers hand in hand –
O'er treetops the errant moon.
Oh, this mad desire to possess!
To waste the soul on blood-red lips.

XII

Sex is a power all cherish,
We worship it on bended knees,
Like old wine it yields the magic
Of oblivion and ecstasies,
The moments drift on golden clouds
To regions of the white beyond.

XIII

Alas, that pleasures never last,
That we must leave the fairy woods
And pass along the great highway.
As much as horizons may beckon,
They flee us the more we pursue
To distances we ne'er can reach.

XIV

The more we give the less we gain –
This is a bitter truth to tell.
Yet passion is a fleeting thing
As flowers wane in summer's heat,
Thus eager kisses, thigh to thigh
Turn phantoms with the colder morn.

XV

Why had you, dearest, to leave me!
Why must friend from friend depart.
Perchance, I shall find the answer
Midst howling winds and rain
Where sombre forests sway and moan
And lightnings stir the darkest lairs.

XVI

Few think they can give without gain,
They attempt to barter with love.
Love comes, it is here, it departs
Leaving wet eyes and broken hearts.
How when we are young can we guess:
Love's winter ne'er returns to spring.

XVII

Love is growth, a wondrous plant
That scatters its seed-pods unseen,
That sheds rarest unknown delights
To those few that worship the dream.
For love squanders all its treasures,
Why should it ask for a return?

XVIII

When youth departs, when love grows dim,
To gray routine hope dwindles down,
Sup well, sit warm, drink deep, sleep sound,
Thus run the hours from the glass.
New vistas beckon here and there
Yet men stay, sullen, where they are.

XIX

Oh, to escape from the city,
Into the blue, shimmering night,
It speaks of all I could have loved,
It speaks of all I longed to see,
To understand, to own, and feel –
Why did so little come to me!

XX

Ah, my fate is not different,
It is like that of all the rest.
There grew flowers at the wayside –
They were mine. I did not cull them.
There were chances made for blessing
When both of us remained unblessed.

XXI

Can a being ever be yours?
Do you know the thoughts of a friend?
Why stray your wishes to strangers
When you own a heart that is true?
Sunlight passes. The night draws near.
Have you been loyal to anyone?

XXII

We reap the harvest that we sow.
Rich crops may sear in rainless heat
Waste over night by wind or frost —
Harsh laws of chance and circumstance!
Yet if your seeds were vain as chaff
Your own will never come to you.

XXIII

Let me pass on to the seashore,
Watch the traverse of white sails,
The seagulls in their spiral flight,
The breakers that brighten the waves,
And as in rambles of boyhood
Fling pebbles out into the sea.

XXIV

They skip o'er the gleaming surface,
They sink and vanish from sight
As all that abides on earth.
Yet on the surface like stray thought,
Each ripple owns an inner sway
And wave-like stirs the azure brine.

XXV

The circle widens, travels farther,
With each emotion keenly felt
Onward it pushes 'cross the waves
Of storm-lashed oceans to unbend
Its tide of beauty on the shore
Of some hope-swept and sun-kissed isle.

XXVI

And there amidst some rarer air
To blossom forth in some great deed –
May it be done by hand or mind –
For the upheaval of the race,
To reach some pinnacle of truth
Where light envelops you and all.

XXVII

This is the land where giant minds,
Vaster than light, vaster than space
Hear whisperings of the infinite,
And with proud sorrow in their eyes,
Their wild-maned coursers ever ready,
Soar far into the skies of thought.

XXVIII

Yet who can follow flights like these,
Who plucks the stars from night's blue vault!
Imagination, sluggish thing,
Will not obey the gayer moods,
Our mind can only peer as far
As fate has lent it eyes to see.

XXIX

Men do not think, they merely dream,
They only long for crude, rough things,
Madly chasing will-o'-the-wisps,
Success by force they to grasp,
It lures them on to wilder scenes
Where wolves in packs hunt dismal prey.

XXX

Why this dull haste, this sordid waste
Of youth and manhood's fullest powers?
To amass riches for your heirs
The highest interests seem low,
And no man's pelf does command health,
Nor can it hold friendship or love.

XXXI

So many do as others do,
They cannot rise from the green mould
With which their thoughts are overgrown.
For them no lotus petals blow,
They peevish bow to any yoke,
And mole-like dig beneath the ground.

XXXII

Thus people born in low estate
Must drag their burden day by day,
'Tis hard to mend what is inborn
And slow the lift to higher planes.
If drudgery rules from morn to night –
They needs must suffer earthly bane.

XXXIII

They stir the coals, press the bellows –
White iron shimmers in the forge
The air is dust, the houses black,
Smoke dragons coil 'round culm and stack
And belch foul breath into the street.
Where is the sun? Has day turned night?

XXXIV

What use to speak to serfs like these
Of odors sweet of new-mown hay,
Red and blue flowers in the wheat,
The old homestead, barns and stables,
Cows shambling home the sunset road –
The angelus over harvest fields.

XXXV

There's joy in labor; so they say,
And well that its praises are sung,
Or mankind in pale-mouthed despair
Would leave factory, forge and shop,
Stead living through their daily toil
Without a thought that death is near.

XXXVI

Afraid of death men do not think
Of their vague meaning on this earth.
Blindly they hope for after-bliss
Or sneer at things they can not guess,
For is not death the cause of all
That ever troubled human brains!

XXXVII

Why do we live, why do we hope,
Why does this world exist at all!
How do we dare to love and mate
When every path is strewn with thorns,
When children share in our fate
And age is glad to greet the night!

XXXVIII

And is it endless sleep and night,
Deliverance or new keen pain?
Hot pitch or stale ambrosia!
There are too many gods adored,
Can one be right, all others wrong –
Who solves the problem why we are?

XXXIX

There is no answer to the quest,
Who knows where we will meet again!
The star realms opening at night
Tell us of other wonder worlds –
Are they spinning through space for us,
Shall we breathe there an ampler air?

XL

Follow yon pilgrims of the East
Through avenues of cypress dim,
Through golden temples, portals red –
Faithful they climb the holy hill
And there confront an empty space
Is that the signet of the grave!

XLI

Some think they know and others doubt,
But who can offer balm to all.
If all were good and fair to meet
No need there be of paradise,
We would not long for other skies
And gather fruit from every tree.

XLII

But what sad use the world has made
Of nature's boundless plenitude,
The frank and free, the sane and true
Are trodden down by foolish crowds.
Greed, barren, shameless, rules supreme,
There is no room for Christ on earth.

XLIII

They dream of universal peace
In times when greed still cruder grows
Than in the days of Skalds and Huns –
Oh, dream of a fraternal race,
Of happiness to all of man!
When will love stronger prove than war!

XLIV

The sword shall break the sword they say,
And force shall strangle force some day.
Thus men march toward battles red,
Their mangled bodies strew the plains,
While o'er the corpse the mother wails,
Her firstborn slain, her pride in life.

XLV

Why should youth be killed from afar,
Races struggle in deadly clutch!
Are no more fallow fields to plough?
Is death's scythe not keen enough!
Oh, mankind, when will you waken
To an honor nobler than death!

XLVI

If no tread of marching armies
Answered a nation's bugle peal,
If young and old refused to bear
Arms 'gainst brethren they do not know,
Then only, in some dim future
May we greet the dawn-doves of peace.

XLVII

One holy war has to be fought –
To make both man and woman free:
The world will flash with signal lights,
Each land ring with its people's voice –
For from those crimson rivulets
Will rise a saner sun-warm life.

XLVIII

For certain things needs must be changed,
Times cannot stay so dull and gray.
Men must rough a freer wind-blown life,
Women no longer shed their bloom
In drudgery for bed and fare,
And children age before their time.

XLIX

Draughts of pure air, bright beams of light
Are free gifts coming from the skies,
Why should sad mothers, children frail
In dark and gruesome hovels pine,
Freeze and starve, and with thirsty eyes
See mirth with song and dance glide by.

L

And hunger is a fearful thing.
It dwarfs the better part in man,
Naught but a withered husk it leaves
Of some thing that should live and breathe.
All nobler impulses turn ghosts,
Haunting waste places of the mind.

LI

It lifts the knife to deadly thrusts,
It turns to brutes all those it sways,
It presses torches into fists,
And peaceful men turn to revolt.
We stand at brinks of volcanoes
Yet smilingly dot them with homes.

LII

What can we do, how can we help!
The poor can never help the poor,
The rich but scatter alms derived
From what is due the common herd,
The weed plots are crowded thick,
Who cuts a path for weary feet!

LIII

Oh, the helplessness of the aged,
Of the needy, sick, and lonely.
Can you explain why they suffer,
Must some lose all while others thrive?
Can no one wear a thornless crown
Without some hurt to human kind?

LIV

Oh, these homes of blighted reason,
Who would not weep at sights like these.
Few years ago they were like us,
They worked and played, they loved and laughed,
And now – beasts without reason;
Where err their erstwhile joys and hopes!

LV

And those who lurk in deadly sin,
Whose book of life reads blood and gold,
Thieves, bandits, outcasts, vagrom folks,
Eternal victims of the law,
Who cannot change, who have no chance
To wash their grimy hands from crime.

LVI

They know not what to do on earth,
Their cup is filled with hate and lust.
None had taught them. Will you teach them?
Have you a larger soul than they?
You have drawn a lucky number,
For them gay fortune went astray.

LVII

In foolish kindness some aspire
To staunch the ever-aching wound,
And so they teach, and so they preach.
How vain to think that your idea
May cure the vanity of things,
'Tis shuttlecock and battledore.

LVIII

How can I give right directions
When I am a wanderer myself!
Onward I stroll and ever on
In my own way courting the sun
And fashioning Arcadia
Of passing winds and flying clouds.

LIX

For my happiness cannot be yours;
In humble ecstasy I could live
In a hill-town, among roses,
With robins feasting at my table,
While woods and fields, valleys and streams
Around would be my promised land.

LX

You might not like such simple fare,
For you the winds may blow too mild –
I cannot tread your well-paved roads
Though verdant they may seem to you.
Each path leads to some point of view,
What you like best, is best for you.

LXI

Sunshine we want but also shadows,
Each joy demands its note of pain,
Each cheek must know the fall of tears
That many dream-swept hopes were vain.
Sorrow digs up unknown treasures
Within the caverns of the mind.

LXII

Have you ever lost a treasure
More precious far than gold or health!
Trailed a white hearse with faltering steps
That bore your dearest dream away,
Sat at the deathbed of your mother,
Or closed a friend's dull staring eyes!

LXIII

You know the frost that chills the core,
That all we love is naught but clay.
Silent a boat glides o'er the Styx,
Yet it leaves light within its wake;
As weary plains grow green with rain
The soul expands in tear-starred nights.

LXIV

Tears furrow thought, they strengthen will,
Cleanse the foul places of the mind,
Yield soothing light to ship-wrecked hearts.
Happy those who, sorrow-driven,
Bright moments wrest from waves of pain
And sail their barks to peaceful ports.

LXV

This is the true philosophy,
Every child may learn the lesson –
Blaze your own trail the best you can
Without trespassing foreign ground;
Smile, play, and sing, and be alive
To every blow of circumstance.

LXVI

To meet the hours as they come,
Salute the days as they pass by,
To bend your neck to no one's yoke,
To be full master of yourself,
To do a kindness when you can –
That is the happiness of life.

LXVII

To help a friend in dire need,
To speak a word to the oppressed,
To think of things that help mankind,
To scatter joy, unasked, unblessed –
For knowing minds divine the rest –
That is the happiness of life.

LXVIII

Yes, life is vain, life is empty,
But why repeat a sad refrain,
The echo of Khayyam's quatrains,
As long as each day has a morrow,
As long as orchards bloom again,
And empty cups may be refilled.

LXIX

Though we recall that days are short,
Let's make the passing moments hum.
Bees do murmur in the heather,
Does sundew exist only for them!
A little joy today seems fairer
Than the brightest strongholds of Spain.

LXX

There are some joys all may attain,
To spouse some cause however slight,
To be a host to loyal friends,
To found some freeholds of your own,
Where mothers laugh and children romp,
And fare in health and fragrance there.

LXXI

Some day religion unbiased
May sponsor stern needs of the day,
Life grow untrammelled and joyous
Without the black magic of law.
Science and art prove their uses
And quicken the heart-beats of all.

LXXII

You, people, come out of your dreams,
Woo fortune and you may win her,
Fill the world with acts of good cheer,
Forget gray cares and ragged toil,
Face bravely the swell and the gale
And strike out for headlands unknown.

LXXIII

Seek beauty and you will find her,
Brave the surge of the crowded street,
Or rest at the mountain's green slope
And commune with trees and the birds,
With the soil and the mossgrown rocks,
And pray at the shrine of the gods.

LXXIV

There are roses and there is youth,
There are joys and sorrows and love,
Dawn and twilight, the noonday sun,
The rolling plains, sky and sea,
None have lost their old-time mystery,
Events pass away, beauty survives.

LXXV

Let us wrest beauty from all there is,
Each and all in their own poor way,
And blithely onward life will flow,
Rare like a long-drawn summer's eve,
And we'll hail and bless each moment
Before it fades into the dark.

JAPANESE RHYTHMS (1933)

Nothing has changed
Since the dusk of the gods —
Drift of water and
Ways of Love —

TANKA I

Winter? Spring? Who knows!
White buds from the plumtrees wing
    And mingle with the snows.
No blue skies these flowers bring
Yet their fragrance augurs spring.

TANKA II

Oh, were the white waves
Far on the glimmering sea
    That the moonshine laves,
Dream flowers drifting to me –
I would cull them, love, for Thee.

TANKA III

Moon, somnolent, white,
Mirrored in a waveless sea,
    What fickle mood of night
Urged thee from heaven to flee
And live in the dawnlit sea!

TANKA IV

　　Like mist on the lees
Fall gently, oh rain of spring
　　On the orange trees
That to Ume's casement cling –
She may hear the lovebird sing.

TANKA V

　　'Though Love has grown cold
The woods are bright with flowers,
　　Why not as of old
Go to the wildwood bowers
And dream of – bygone hours!

TANKA VI

　　Tell what name beseems
These vain and wandering days!
　　Like the bark of dreams
That from souls at daybreak strays
They are lost on trackless ways.

TANKA VII

　　Oh, climb to my lips
Frail muse of the amber wine!
　　Joy to him who sips
Cups of steaming sake wine
Rising from some source divine!

TANKA VIII

If pleasures be mine
As aeons and aeons roll by,
   Why should I repine
That under some future sky
I may sport as butterfly?

TANKA IX

Dew and dawn flowers
Doomed both to flutter astray
   – Through the noon hours –
Will the flowers dewless sway
Or their petals strew the way?

TANKA X

Just three words to say :
I love you! No more! No less!
   Hard I tried today –
Why should it cause such distress
To utter words that confess!

TANKA XI

Were we able to tell
When Old Age would come our way
   We would muffle the bell,
Lock the door and steal away –
Let him call some other day!

TANKA XII

Moonlight! There is none.
Springtime! Where are thy flowers
I can see not one.
The scenes we knew seem estranged –
How remained my love unchanged!

TANKA XIII

Thousand years may pass
Till this fir bends to decay –
Fair morning glory
Content with a single day,
Do you mourn your shorter stay?

TANKA XIV

The sky is a sea,
Where white clouds like billows play
And the moon a boat
Oaring through the Milky Way
To some star-reef far away!

TANKA XV

Not yet has faded
The wealth of cherry flowers –
Wind, hasten their doom
Make them rain in pink showers
While our love is in bloom!

TANKA XVI

Tell me, autumn night
What is perturbing my mind.
    Is it that I wait
For One who does not come
Or is it the moan of the wind!

TANKA XVII

Who could it have been
That gave Love its misleading
    Superfluous name!
To call love 'death' would be plain
They mean so often the same.

TANKA XVIII

Endless hours of strife
Troubles drear of household life
    Landlord, child, and wife –
They thronged like bills in arrears
Last night's dream of fifty years.

TANKA XIX

When I close the gate
Seasons for a new master
    This old shack may wait –
Oh plumtree, grazing the eaves
In spring bloom never be late.

TANKA XX

So eager to live!
How patiently, dear, you watched
    For the first warm day
Rain mists still blurring the view
Now also will clear away.

(to a convalescent)

HAIKAI I

White petals afloat
On a winding woodland stream –
    What else is life's dream!

HAIKAI II

Butterflies a–wing
Are you flowers returning
    To your branch in spring?

HAIKAI III

Rainy days in spring –
Frogs splash in the lotus pond –
    Hear the waters sing!

HAIKAI IV

At new moon we met!
Two weeks I've waited in vain
    Tonight! Don't forget!

HAIKAI V

Oh, red maple leaves
There are more of you these eves
    Than ever grew on trees!

HAIKAI VI

   In May who can say
Is it Uyeno's bell
   Or Asakusa's! *
      (*two temples in Kyoto surrounded by cherry trees)

HAIKAI VII

   What mortal can write
Of the blossoms' dawn-rose flight
   Down Yoshino Mount!

HAIKAI VIII

   If all the year round
With blossoms the hills were white
   Would they seem as bright?

HAIKAI IX

   On the barren cliff
The fir for her roots finds room –
   Love on less may bloom.

HAIKAI X

   Have all leaves turned red
Has summer past to tell me
   That my youth has fled?

HAIKAI XI

   If herons could fly
Noiselessly across the sky
   They would look like snow.

HAIKAI XII

And saddest of all
Fusiyama changed its shape –
   Drape the world in crepe!
     (*after the 1923 earthquake*)

HAIKAI XIII

   Why, black crow, alight
On the fir tree's withered branch
   On this autumn night?

HAIKAI XIV

   Eyes foresee at noon
Your beauty – oh Miidera (temple)
   Courted by the moon!

HAIKAI XV

   At daybreak I wake
And lo! wisterias hang
   Deep into the lake.

HAIKAI XVI

   The bucket quite dry
And weed-bloom choking my well!
   Where's water nearby?

HAIKAI XVII

   What holds life for me
On the plumtrees but one
   Butterfly I see.

DODOITSU I

'Love drifts astray with the years'
I muse under pine trees tall –
Are my cheeks suffused with tears
  Or does the dew fall?

DODOITSU II

As a waterweed drifting –
Finds no place to bloom and stay
Also we forever shifting
  Know for Truth no way.

DODOITSU III

Sun and mist in the orchard
Flowers of plum, peach, and pear
Which of the three, I wonder
  Choicest fruit will bear?

DODOITSU IV

Oh fragrant breeze of the night
Blow from the heather, greet the
'Two firs that age together'
  And yield us delight!

THE JAPANESE CONCEPTION OF POETRY (1904)

At a time when everything in Western literature tends towards brevity of expression, it may be interesting to examine a literature which, in its poetry at least, has already adhered to the principles of concentration.

Japanese poetry claims this distinction. It is absolutely confined to lyrical effusions of the utmost brevity. The Japanese poem is generally limited to three, four or five lines, and seldom exceeds a few dozen. One would look in vain for a poem of the length of Bryant's 'Thanatopsis'. Japanese literature has never invaded the epic field, and knows no metrical form which even remotely resembles an ode, a ballad, or a long poetic narrative like 'The Ancient Mariner'. Also minor metrical arrangements like the rondel, triolet, villanelle, etc., are absent.

Of what, then, does Japanese poetry consist? If one discusses its apparent lack of scope and resources with a Japanese, he is sure to point to the 'Mayōshiu Kogi' (Collection of Myriad Leaves). True enough, its bulkiness is almost alarming, as it extends to 122 volumes. But it proves to be only an anthology of short poems, each complete, bearing no relation to other stanzas, except in the choice of subject; the work being divided into poems of Spring, Summer, Autumn, Winter; poems of Parting, Love, Sorrow, etc. Collections of this kind, admirably printed and supplied with numerous indexes and elaborate commentaries, are published, at intervals, under the auspices of the government. They represent the classical poetry of Japan. The metrical forms most often encountered are those of the *tanka* and *haikai*.

The *tanka* is a rhythmical construction of five lines of 5, 7, 5, 7 and 7 syllables. To write a poem within the compass of thirty-one syllables or a dozen words, as the Japanese language is even more polysyllabic than those of Anglo-Saxon origin, would seem to us a most difficult task. But the Japanese do not enjoy in vain the reputation of being dainty in all their aesthetic accomplishments, and the same exquisite workmanship displayed in their netsukes and hammered bronzes can be found in the *tanka*. It is astonishing what a wealth of word pictures, what elegant phrasing and rhythmical shading, what subtle sentiments and thoughts can be compressed into these lyrical epigrams.

The following – a *tanka* that has won its way to the hearts of every one – may be taken as characteristic of the vague and dreamy, and yet so suggestive style of Japanese poetry:

Moonshine! There is none:
Springtime! Where are its flowers!
Spring seems to be gone:
All life is estranged, my love
Alone has remained unchanged.

The poem explains itself. The poetess returning to the place where her lover has met the previous spring, finds it sadly changed. As in former days the moon and the flowers greet her eyes, but in a feeling of despair she denies even their existence and plunges into melancholy musings at the sight of the familiar scenes.

The translation is as nearly as possible literal, endeavoring at the same time to imitate some rhythmical peculiarities. Also the original has the reiteration of 'shine' and 'time,' repeats the word 'spring' in the third line, and has the same ending for the second and third line. Any attempt, however, to convey the euphony and the rhythmic beauty of Japanese poem into a foreign tongue, is futile.

The language, having no affinity to the Aryan family nor to any other Asiatic tongue, but standing by itself, despite certain Chinese influences, does not adapt itself to translation. Its syllabary has neither diphthongs, combinations of consonants, nor final consonants; but consists exclusively of single vowels, or consonants followed by a vowel. These peculiarities not only lend the language a peculiar sound, full of unexpected modulations – minor scales, blurred and rapid like some Eastern music, made for the soul of a different humanity – but deprive its metrical forms of rhymes as well as measure. As there are only five vowels, and every word ends in a vowel, it can be readily understood that the poet would have merely five rhymes at his command. Consequently rhyming in our Western sense is unknown. It occurs only accidentally, as for the sake of rhythm at the endings and the metrical breaks of verses. The absence of measure is largely due to the peculiar careless manner in which the Japanese accentuate their words. They talk rapidly, and slur over the transition from one word to another.

The regular succession of accented and unaccented syllables exists in their language as well as ours, but in speech almost disappears. The two syllabled words generally have the accent on the final, the three, four and five syllabled ones on the second, and all imperative forms and present participles on the last syllable. This would afford ample opportunity for a skilful combination of trochaic and dactylic measures, but the Japanese poets have never indulged in such metrical devices. The shortness of their lines rendered the introduction of poetical feet unprofitable.

They apply a certain parallelism between nouns and verbs of two successive lines, as, for instance:

129

Met the gods in high assembly,
Met the gods and held high counsels,

a device familiar to us from the Psalms, and from parallel lines in Thomas Hood, Longfellow, Poe and other poets. But the Japanese gains little by this occasional ornament, the equal length of all syllables prevents any startling sound-recurrence. The only ambition of the *tanka* writers is to make every poem a *rhythmic* whole, an expression of fresh and unconscious modulation. The subject itself – be it a wall of rippling wisteria or the undulations of a tree trunk – has to suggest the rhythm most suitable for the interpretation. And as the open vowel sounds permit an endless variety of modulation, and as there are no metrical rules, it is really nothing but a primitive application of the *vers libre*.

The mechanism is really of primitive naturalness. And yet in a way nothing more perfect and complete than these little poems can be imagined. The alternation of lines of five and seven syllables, the improvisation of rhythm, and the exclusive application of the so-called classic style, which prohibits words of Chinese derivation and all colloquial expressions, are obeyed scrupulously. There has never existed a word-arrangement which, despite its apparent looseness, has remained so firm in construction and so decided in purpose through centuries of use.

The themes considered suitable for interpretation are dictated by tradition. They are limited to 'lyrical' emotions. Opening the *Book of Myriad Leaves* we undergo the experience Lowell had as he became acquainted with Raynouard's Provencal anthology: 'We are deafened and confused by a hundred minstrels singing the same song at once.' The classic poets of Japan deliberately refrain from didacticism and satire. Even the glorification of war, which plays such a conspicuous part in their dramas and novels, seems to contain no poetical element for them. There are no angers, despairs, enthusiasms, hatreds, violent emotions of any sort, in their stanzas. They are no banner-bearers of revolt or reform. Their muse is one of calm. It deals only with personal and momentary moods, expressed in mellifluent metaphors and crystalline imagery, in a language, vital and dignified, incapable of conveying the intricacies of speculative thought or a direct enunciation of ideas, but exactly fashioned to suggest a picture and a vague emotion. They have amatory verses, which faintly resemble Herrick, poems of sadness and longing, not unlike Heine minus his irony, fervent praises of women and wine of which Anacreon would not be ashamed, and lamentations over the the uncertainties of life which sound like a faint echo of Omar Khayyam's rose-scented quatrains.

The leading characteristic of the Japanese poet seems to be his fertile fancy for pictorial minuteness. Nature is always the leading *motif*. All his metaphors are drawn from the external beauties of nature. The moon is a bark oaring its way to the grove of the stars; sporting butterflies resemble fallen flowers that return to their branches; he wishes that the white breakers far out in the sea were flowers that would drift to his lady love; and asks the fir-clad cliffs at the seashore how many wet wave garments they have worn. The sight of two old fir trees suggests to him a married couple growing old together. He never tires of depicting the four seasons in all their aspects. The partiality of our Western poets for twilight and starlit nights he, however, does not share. But these curious omissions are exceptions. Nearly everything in nature interests him. The hazes and 'ice thaws' which usher in the spring, the sound of falling leaves on an autumn evening, the sough of wind in the reeds at the edge of the marshes, the vision of the snow-covered summits of Fuji, or fir-clad cliffs glimmering out to sea, are some of the subjects the Japanese poet always like to dwell upon. There is no flower blooming in Japan which has not received adequate poetic treatment, and one might assert that at least one-fourth of all poems mention either the cherry flowers, the wisteria, the peony, the convolvulus, or the vari-colored blossoms of the plum tree which exhale their perfume in the snow and frost and 'make us think longingly of the past.'

Like the Japanese painter, who excels in expressing the attitudes and motion of fish and fowl, and, above all, the sportive grace of little forest creatures, like the squirrel, the poet also finds inspiration in the leaping of a trout in a mountain stream, the lines of wild geese making a dark streak across the sky, even in the croaking of a frog among lotus leaves, or the chirruping of insects in the undergrowth. His admiration of nature even goes so far as to compare one aspect of it with another. A Western poet wandering through a pine forest at night, and suddenly perceiving in the utter darkness a gleam of silver light, might compare the moon shining to some fairy palace with glittering window panes; in short, to some object of his experience or imagination; the Japanese poet, on the other hand, would compare the glimmering light to 'a moonlit crag of Fusiyama.'

The Japanese always remains an observer. He never becomes one with nature. He does not possess the faculty of endowing inanimate objects with life. To invest clouds and woods with human thoughts and desires, as, for instance, Shelley has done, seems bald and meaningless to him, and such a sentence as 'Aurora, veiling herself in clouds, like a blushing girl' he would consider in very bad taste. He looks at the world with the eyes of an ideal realist, or rather of an impressionist. Life passes, like the dissolving views of a magic lantern, showing one beautiful landscape after the other, each one containing sufficient material for an exquisite vignette.

For centuries the *tanka* which, according to Japanese belief was already in use in prehistoric times, reigned supreme. It had caught the ear of the public, and apparently satisfied all lyrical aspirations. No innovation was attempted. At last in the sixteenth century a serious rival, in shape of a still shorter poem, the *haikai*, made its appearance. If the term lyrical epigram is appropriate for the brevity and metrical limitations of the *tanka*, the *haikai* should be a called a 'lyrical aphorism'. Its brevity seems artificial and exaggerated. Seventeen syllables – three lines of 5, 7, 5 syllables – are all the resources a writer has to produce a word-picture. It is a mode of expression which necessarily had to deteriorate into mere exclamations, and there are actually poems of this kind which consist merely of four or five words. Moreover, a certain compound adjective, the 'pillow-word', is used, a survival from the archaic stages of the language. The mountains are 'mist enshrouded' or 'dotted with monasteries', the fall moon 'soul-contenting', the cherry blossoms 'drenched with spring rain' etc. And as these epithets convey to the native reader a deeper meaning than meets our ear, and as these words are invariably five syllables long, they form a most valuable vehicle for concise expression.

The *haikai*, however, differs from the *tanka* in more than the number of lines. It has less choice in diction, and deals at times with humorous and frivolous subjects, which the older kind of poetry refuses to meddle with. But it enriched the vocabulary by the adoption of large numbers of Chinese words, and acquired a clearness and directness unattainable with the more cumbrous expressions of the classic style.

A typical *haikai* is the following one:

A cloud of (cherry) flowers!
Is it Uyeno's bell
Or Asakusa's?

To the Japanese student these lines convey a perfect picture. The famous temples of Uyeno and of Asakusa in the vicinity of Yeddo are surrounded by a belt of cherry trees, whose blossoms form a perfect wall in spring, shutting them entirely out of view. And the passer-by does not know whether the bell of Uyeno or Asakusa is ringing. Suggestiveness like this can hardly be excelled. Nothing but the most essential is expressed. It is very much like the Japanese watercolorist, who expresses by one dash of his brush a swallow in full flight, or suggests, by an angle of lines with a half circle behind, the autumn moon rising among the hills. To our Western mind this impressionism which seems more remarkable for what it does not represent than what it does, is often obscurely allusive. It transcends our comprehension. We want passages of pathos that draw tears, sublime utterances that overawe our soul, and humorous conceits that draw laughter. We want a finished picture – not a vision without shadows and perspective – a true poetic expression, quite independent of the verbal melody, perfectly expressed in regard to style and form.

The Japanese reader agrees with us that emotion is the true basis of all poetic expression, but he wants merely a suggestion to convey to the sketchy outlines of the poet's conception his own poetic imagination, and the emotions that are stirred within his own breast.

How much confidence the Japanese poet has in his readers is astonishing. Frequently he does not even find it necessary to attach a sentiment to his word pictures. He simply depicts a crow sitting on a withered branch, and leaves it to the reader to add the poetic thought. If he wants to dwell upon the fugitiveness of all earthly things he simply says, 'A joint of bamboo is floating down the river'; if he wants to compare the sorrows of mankind with fading autumn leaves that cover the ground, he exclaims, 'There are far more of you than ever I saw growing on the trees!' And the melancholy despair of two lovers, whose passion has subsided, he expresses by a single image. When the lovers' passion was at its height, they swore that they would love each other as long as the smoke should rise from Mount Fuji. The poet, however, deems it unnecessary to make this explanation, he finds it amply sufficient to express this complex emotion, to which Swinburne has devoted hundreds of lines in his 'Félise', by one short, sharply-defined sentence, 'The smoke no longer rises from Mount Fuji.'

The symbolism of Japanese poetry is unique. It has nothing in common with our Western emblematic signs and forms. It is rather a spiritual idea, a subtle speculation, a unison of the external beauties of nature and the subtleties of the human soul, which has its origin in tradition and a continual association with flowers, with animals, trees, and mountains and the ever-changing elements. Every glimpse of nature is endowed with a symbol, a hidden meaning to all who know the magic password. In this graphic symbolism exists for the initiated the greatest charm of Japanese poetry.

It may be interesting to investigate how this singular terseness, this love for reduction, condensation and fragmentary beauty came into Japanese literature.

The writing of poetry is no profession in Japan. The poets were mostly courtiers or ladies of the leisure classes, who took up verse-making as a pastime. Nearly every well-bred person can improvise a *tanka*. The mother of the writer, like most Japanese young ladies, whose education consists largely of writing, music, and the study of the various anthologies, could paint fairly well and indite an original stanza upon occasion.

Much of the poetry was the outcome of poetical tournaments, at which themes were proposed by judges; and each phrase and word was examined with the minutest care before the verdict was pronounced. And as hundreds of poets and poetesses took part in these competitions, of which two were annually held at the imperial court, it can be imagined that short poems were in favor. They did not take poetry so seriously as we do; to them it was merely a substitute for a cup of thick *sake* or for the few whiffs of which a Japanese smoke consists. They looked at literature as a sport, and diverted themselves by stringing a few 'silver phrases' together – a game like any other. True enough, they were experts in the game, their rhythmic caprices were always perfect in form, but they refrained form unnecessary technical difficulties, and left the choice of more important subjects to the novelist and dramatist. They merely wished to lend expression to a passing fancy, and they found the *tanka* a most suitable form. The subtlety of sentiment is largely due to feminine participation. A large part of Japanese poetry was written by women, and their life among a few gems of bric-à-brac, among flowers arranged according to certain canons of beauty, and their miniature gardens, which demanded infinite care, all tended toward a miniature art.

Writing for leisure and guided by an exquisite taste, they never published their effusions – volumes of poetry by an individual writer are almost unknown – they wisely left the responsibility of selection and the cares of publication to the government, which took a pride in issuing anthologies. The poet was apparently of the opinion that the 'less literary baggage he took with him the more certain he was of travelling safely down the roads of fame.' If a writer was represented by more than thirty stanzas he was considered a writer 'whose fragrant name was known to all the world.'

Three other metrical forms have still be investigated. They are the *na–ga–uta*, the 'long' poem, the *hanka*, a sort of envoi attached to other poems, and the *kioka*, the comic verse.

The *na–ga–utas* are very scarce. The *Kokinshiu*, an anthology of over eleven hundred ancient and modern poems, contains only five specimens. Metrically they are really nothing but several *tanka* strung together with a regular alteration of five- and seven-syllabled phrases. Foreign readers will not find much to interest them in these short narratives. Even the reader who has a competent knowledge of the language requires a special study of mythology and Japanese society to understand and appreciate them. A peculiarity of the long poem is the application of the 'pivot-word', which is strictly prohibited to the *tanka* and *haikai* writers. It is a word which has two meanings, and which is used in a way that it makes sense with the preceding as well as the following sentence. It is a most extravagant form of verbal embellishment. One may smile at a conceit like the following:

```
        night
The knight } rose from the couch at
        dawn
    Don } ned his armor and sallied forth,
```

but if continued through an entire poem it becomes unbearable. It is also one of the reasons why Japanese poetry has never found an Edward FitzGerald. A poem interspersed with pivot-words is simply untranslatable.

The *hanka* is a short poem of thirty-one syllables in four lines. It is never used as an independent poem, but invariably as a feature of the long poem. Unlike envoi, it is not addressed to any art patron, high dignitary or symbolical personage, but is in most cases simply an echo of the principal idea of the poem or a commentary on the leading event or character.

The *kioka* is a variety of the *tanka*. Its principal object is to make people laugh, and absolute liberties in regard to language and choice of subjects are taken. The language, although irresistibly funny to the native, is often extremely improper. Ordinary poems and acrostics, pillow-words and pivot-words, and other contortions of speech are used with an exasperating lavishness.

The introduction of Western ideas has also changed Japanese poetry to some extent. The study of Western literature was introduced, and Shakespeare, Gray, Campbell, Longfellow and other poets have been translated in parts. A more important consideration still is the stimulus which the language itself derived from a more thorough assimilation of Chinese elements, a movement which began as far back as the sixteenth century. The revolt was against classicisms of native origin, which had become largely unintelligible to the public, and the return to the purity of the Chinese classics, which reveal a larger vocabulary, a simpler grammatical system and a greater wealth of phonetic resources. Chinese words now far outnumber those of native origin.

A new school of poetry, which took up European and American writers as models sprang up in the eighties. They still write *na-ga-utas*, but divide them like our ballads into stanzas of equal length. They retain the old principle of lines of five and seven syllables, but begin with the seven-syllable phrase. Finding the classical language unequal to the expression of new ideas, they make free use of the colloquial, which hitherto had been only used in the *kioka*. Toyoma, the chief originator of the movement, has published a poem on the great earthquake of 1855. It is narrated in a grand style, with a fullness of detail hitherto unknown in Japan. The only fault is that it lacks local color; it is genuine poetry, but poetry in the Western sense which might just as well have a Campbell or Freiligrath as author. The majority of poems of this school have the same defect. They have, however, attracted much attention, and given rise to a lively controversy between adherents of the old and new styles. Although the *tanka* and the *haikai* are still the most favored and characteristic forms, it cannot be denied that the movement has endowed Japanese poetry with new and rich resources. If, without abandoning the modern standpoint it will still be able to adhere to its classic principles, to the truthfulness of its similes and metaphors, to its love of nature and free and spontaneous expression of emotion, the all-pervading suggestiveness of Japanese art will speak to us with renewed vigor and with more eloquence than it hitherto has spoken.

MISCELLANEOUS POEMS FROM PERIODICALS AND MANUSCRIPTS (1886–1944)

UNTITLED

    If words of mine
    Own strength to live
Centuries hence, man's mind
May tune in on their scatter and drift –
That is as long as a house of art
Stands bright and bold
    On windswept heights
    And waves will cradle
Smiles of generous stars
       On ebon nights.

TO MY MOTHER[*]

A woman's death created me, must therefore not
My love hang over all the world! – Poor mother, my life shall expiate thy premature demise.

Rest with my thanks, rest softly under the hills
Of Kobe, under the hills of thy native land!
May nature's gifts exult to beautify thy grave,
While winds and birds sing everlasting funeral
Rites to thee, my mother dear.

The day will come when I shall kiss that sacred soil,
And to the floweriness that from thy ashes rose,
Each kiss shall tell the secret of my life: 'To
Thee I owe what I may give of Beauty to this world.'

(1887)

---

[*] Hartmann wrote the following in 1922, which he called 'criticism': This poem appears
to me now, as most effusions of that period, a trifle early-ripe, touched as it were by German middle-class sentimentality. As we grow older we are apt to look with a feeling of
superiority and tolerance at the actions of youth – wrongly so. Whatever the callowness of
youthful expression may utter, it has at least the merit of genuineness. Its altruistic quality
is an honest overflow of sentiment, not yet trimmed like boxwood in a gentleman's garden. A little more of the original vernal sap would add a desirable flavor to our later days'
accomplishments.

Sorry to state that the material in this instance was unfortunately chosen. As I learnt
later, my mother was not buried at all. As she was a Buddhist and had associated with a
foreigner she was by some 'churlish priest' refused burial in that beautiful hill cemetery at
Nagasaki, where one might want to sleep forever, if one occasionally could peep out of
the earth and glance over the glorious bay and harbour scene. If roundabout information
can be trusted, she was cremated on some by-way near Kobe, and her ashes then and there
were scattered to the winds, to whiten some sinuous mountain path to this very day.

The saddest of all this matter is that I have never been able to greet the land of my birth
except in waking dreams and excursions into Japanese poetry. Will my fate be like that
of the author of 'Wilhelm Tell,' never to see the country which he most longed to visit?

FRAGMENT

In silence we sat together,
In silence we fell asleep
Like flowers in dreamland weather
Thro' which the night winds creep.

THE JASMINE FLOWER

See this branch of sweetest flowers
Plucked at morn from dewy bowers
Sent with love to greet me
Breathing friendship sweet.

THE LOOM SONG

The light of the fireflies glows as they play
While the loom is being set to weave today
Five rolls of linen must be done by tonight
Green for my teacher, lavender for my family,
Black for my brother-in-law, Red for my father-in-law,
Yellow for the Emperor, and all must be done by tonight.

UNTITLED

East, west, north or south
Send forth a favoring gale
Now on the stately ship
The gods of fortune sail

Great prosperity, great success,
In all you hope to do
May the smiling gods bestow
These gracious gifts on you.

THE MELTING POT

Hunky, Polak, Kike, and Jap,
Nigger, Greaser, Chink, and Wop,
Double, double, boil and trouble,
Fire burn and cauldron bubble,
In this cauldron bake and boil!

FRAGMENT

> If my mother had known
> That such things can be
> She would have refrained from the pleasure
> Of giving birth to me
yodolee – lodolee – i – o – yoohoo!

MORNING DREAMS
To Alice O'Donnell

Alice, dost thou still remember the time now long, long
past, when we two were straying through the gardens of
the universe, when birds were fluttering 'round us and
sang mysterious songs, when all the flowers of the field
kissed our feet to greet our golden days of innocence,
when loving words were lingering in the flowery glades,
and visions rose from out the shade?

Oh, still I hear thy clear voice ringing like chimes
through the silent air, and still I see thy laughing
eyes, and flaunting hair caressed by the evening winds.
Our words were poems and our feelings songs!

But also we, *we* had to part; we each have said Farewell!
We did not weep, we did not think of love. And yet thy
lips did breathe a prayer and sank on mine; and when I
felt the last press of thy loving hand my hands were
moist with tears. Ah, love, thou sweet religion of the
universe, thou wast the under-dream of every thought.

Alice, how strange is human life! So many hopes fly
silently away, and only their recollections still touch
our mellow hearts. Where art thou now, sweet comrade
of my childhood days? Does thy beauty still rest in
sunny realms, or is thy spring bedimmed with tears like mine?

When shall I look again into your face? Or shall we
never meet again? And hast thou only meteor-like rushed
through my dreams of hope? (1886)

THE CONVALESCENT GIRL
wasted blossoms of 86/87 to Emma Willers

How soon the ninety days of the Spring will pass!
Of ten, nine trees have lost their blossoms.
How could it be otherwise, after so much rain and storm.
But I do not believe that beautiful days come seldom
    after spring.

How well I can study nature from my open window.
And what do I see?

The butterflies feeling a little weak after the rain,
    flutter about in the mild and golden atmosphere.
The bees hover around the clover in the lawn.
The swallows build their nests on their roof of our house,
    and in the corner of the garden the spider
    catches the falling blossoms in her web.
And you, little insect, why do you come to me instead of
    playing among the flowers that were made of you?

What sounds are those? Ah, it is Willie playing the
    melodies I like.

At last, tired of looking and listening, I open the
    Great Book and try to solve the essence of all the
    mysteries around.

(1886)

TO WALT WHITMAN

Poet of America! The language of thy songs is rough,
but its natural sternness penetrates to the soul, and is the
harbinger of a new poetry, and a higher school of art than
even that of Greece.

Renovator of glories, past and forgotten! Prophet of
grand futures, of sacred unions, and true democracies!
Exposer of existing wrongs, pleader for reform, longing
for a race of independent men and women of moral
strength and religiousness; for happier domestic lives,
worthy of the eternal soul of earthly pioneers. Manliest
man, not ashamed of doing any kind of work, thy callest
every honest occupation good and grand.

Listening patiently to the voice of common people, not
excluding prostitutes, with faith in mankind, knowing
their good and bad, thou believest in progress, and
becomest the companion of all souls traveling on the
road of the universe. Thou lighten'st the burdens, thou
lessen'st the cares of thy comrades, and givest freely alms,
being poor thyself. Oh, would all men taste only once in
their life the joy of self-sacrifice, which thou hast felt in
nursing for many a year the sick and wounded soldiers of
the Secession War.

Adorer of all organic beauties; thy God is no science,
no sickly doubt, but nature's evangelism; the solitude
is to thee a place more fit for devotion than illuminated
sanctuaries, tabernacles, and altars.

Friend of youth, maturity, and age, thou see'st in babes
sucking their mother's breasts the heroes and bards
of ages to come. Boldly revealing the joys of sexual
intercourse, thou proudly assertest that the seminal fluid
of a perfect father is the very essence of life, and that
upon the wombs of perfect mothers the future and the
happiness of the world depend. (Genuine womanhood,
press an ardent kiss upon the bare breast of him who
glorifies life's mysteries.)

Thy truths need no protector, time will prove their best
apostle. If our generation cannot rise to thy spiritual and
moral purity, our children will be able to honor thy life,
hallowed by Virginia's battlefields; and posterity will
remember thee as one of the best and greatest men, which
America, which the world produced.

Lover of mankind, sending to all brethren the kiss of
divine fraternity, will thy dazzling dream of universal
harmony be ever realized? – If every man and woman
were as satisfied with life as thou art, then, much were
gained; life would be, indeed, a paradise.

Walt Whitman, I do not call thee master, but I am bound
to thee forever, thy works were to me, except Love and
Nature, the grandest lessons of my life.

Thou art to me like a star of promise, to whom I gaze
at midnight, who tells me of other globes sweeping
through the universe. My heart aches with delirious joys,
my limbs tremble, and I would kneel to thee, beautiful
orb, if I did not feel that also my soul is a part of that
incomprehensible totality which creates and maintains.

IDEALISM

A young poet was pondering on the destiny of man. He
rose and shouted, his eyes like lightning blazing, into
the darkness of the world:
   'May be heretofore not much good has been done,
   but the time will come, the time will surely
   come, when man will do good just for the sake
   of doing it!'
Time stopped a moment in her furious run and grimly smiling
inquired, 'When?'
The Future turned over the leaves in the Book of the Universe
and doubtfully murmured, 'Not in the next millennium!'
At last the Goddess of Truth imperiously rose and thundered
forth, 'Never!'
   The young poet had listened to every word. He smiled
   and simply repeated: 'The time will come, the time
   will surely come, when man will do good just for the
   sake of doing good.'

(1886)

BOTH CALLED ME 'LOVE'

Both called me 'love' in a sweet low voice, as
I held them in my arm, the sea was softly gleaming, the night was bright and warm.
One of the elves had golden hair and her eyes were clear
and blue; the other owned two soft brown stars and tresses
of auburn hue.

Their cheeks were blushing gently like roseleaves floating
on milk, and their delicate limbs were glowing in robes of
daintiest silk.
I loved them both and knew not to whom I should
promise my hand; so I kissed them both and
left for a foreign land.

(1890)

NIGHT OF LOVE

I gallop along a deserted road
   To the right side lies the beach
   To the left are barren fields
   As far as the eye can reach.

Above me the sparkling heaven
   Around me the silence of night
   My horse and I dash forwards
   To a distant flickering light.

There waits a brown-eyed maiden
   For her lover's wild embrace
   She stands at the door and listens
   To the sounds that travel through space.

(1891)

ONCE I MET AN INNOCENT GIRL

Once I met an innocent girl slumbering under an
oak tree's shade, far away from highway and cottage.
She was dreaming a dream of innocence at the bank
of the murmuring brook, her hair still bedewed with
the glittering wet.

I softly knelt down and gazed at her angel-like limbs,
while two little birds were twittering a carol of hope
and of bliss; and holding my breath, I pressed a kiss
on her half-opened lips and felt as dead, in paradise.

Suddenly I looked at my garments, and reality rough
and cold had seized me again. I hastily rose while
a tear fell gently upon her breast.

(1887)

SUGGESTIONS

The coffin was wooden and black;
the clothes of the girl in rags.
No friends had come to mourn her fate.
One of the undertakers roughly said:
'You ask why she killed herself! Her
lover left her, and then – you know
the rest.'

I stood at the coffin for a long long time.
I looked at the painful smile on her lips,
and bending over her rigid marble limbs
once so full of life, I murmured:
'It is better so,' and kissed the pale
cold forehead of murdered innocence.

I left the cottage and outside the horizon
was fairly aglow with purple clouds.
I saw a pair of lovers under the elder tree.

Late in the evening when passing by
to seek my humble home, they still were
there in the balmy light of the moon.

(1887)

TEACHERS

Have you said farewell to the dominions of Philistia forever?

Does your way of teaching develop the body, mind, emotion?

Can you speak of the victory of purity over the temptations
  of egotism?

Are you able to be impartial?

Are neither a bigot nor an atheist?

Have you a general idea about all things?

Do you remember that notions about history and the capacity
of solving mathematical problems are no dire necessities?

Do you know some things about the intricacies of macrocosm
and microcosm?

Are you a lover of men?

Do you comprehend the poetry of nature and life and beauty of
art?

Have you formed in your mind an idea of the laws, harmonies,
mysteries of the universe? Have you thought of the eternity of
molecules, of the destiny of the world? Have you studied the
organism of man, the influence of maladies and nervousness?
Have you considered that individuals form a nation, form
a race? Are you familiar with the effects of enthusiasm,
talents, genius? Do you know what passions, instincts, moods,

impressions are? Do you know something about the unconscious change of feelings? Are you really able to teach your pupils to become strong personalities, that they may bid defiance to all variations and influences, that they must trust their own forces and faculties, that they may be able to enjoy this world?

Teachers, answer these questions. Young teachers, you must be able to answer everyone of them, for life or death, unto eternity and ever widening circles of the world, centers in these hundred human brains there that you have to educate.

(1887)

TO PHILOSOPHERS

Plato and all ye famous and illustrious men
of the past, men whose words, whose virtue
and whose deeds have survived centuries of
agitation, and who still live in the thoughts
and meditations of today – to you my thanks,
to you salutation of my mind.

Yet of your influence here among us, I have
not much to tell, friends of my intellect.
It only pains my inmost soul, when I reflect
on the trifling success of your works for good.
For if your ideas had been realized, even the
bold ideas of a single one of you, lament
would be no longer the first word and the
last of man.

(1886)

FINITA COMMEDIA
To T. V. Chominski

I dreamt last night that I was dead and awakening
after one thousand years from a cold and silent
sleep, I saw before me the City of New York, a
range of towering stone, monstrous, sunlit, in all
her midday glory – infested by little black ants
running to and fro.

Another thousand years swept by; I awoke once more, the City lay
there, a Babel lost in earth and clouds, a twilight world,
more gaunt and ominous than before – still infested by little
black ants rushing to and fro.

Again I fell to sleep. I do not know for how many
thousand years, when I awoke all was dark and void, and
asking, 'Where is the City of New York!' the moon broke
through the clouds and cast her weird gray light on
the ruins of a city – country – race – what has
become of the frantic little black ants that rushed so
frantically to and fro!

(1889)

CATHEDRAL SACRILEGE

A silken hose in a golden haze
An opening rose in a maze of lace
A color dream in marmorean whiteness
A sensual gleam in subdued brightness
   And my languid soul
   In a mild vibration
   Embraces the nude
   In a wild violation.

(1892)

GROUND FOG

Weird to walk through the mist
Ghost every tree and stone
No house can see its neighbor
You near yet I feel lone

Day is proud with pleasure
When shadows strengthen light
Who lifts a hidden treasure
When mist veils flutter night

In a shifting world of phantoms
Who guesses the right way
The best life should enlist
This drifting grayness cuts away

Weird to walk through the mist
To see neither lane nor wall
No being knoweth another
Ground fog enshrouds us all

Of familiar scenes no trace
Where are your hands – your face
Are we lost in a maze
Beyond earth, time and space

RAIN (PANTOUM)

Spears of white rain come hurtling down
Piercing with new life the garden grounds,
Breaking the mist curves on the marshed brown
To the strange patter of harpstring sounds.

   Piercing with white spears the garden grounds
   Blurring the shapes of field and home,
   With the strange patter of harpstring sounds
   Vague thoughts are stirred and start to roam.

Blurring the shapes of field and home –
Ghosts of wishes, forlorn and shy –
Frail thoughts awaken and start to roam,
A sadness seems to fall from the sky.

   Why these desires forlorn and shy!
   Why this tat-pat on eave and sill!
   A sadness seems to fall from the sky
   Blotting out distant wood and hill.

Why this tat-pat on eave and sill
Curtaining the world to an humbler place,
Blotting out distant wood and hill,
Carrying dreams into wide wan space.

   Narrowing the world to a humbler place
   As we stare through the chill wet pane,
   Sending our dreams into wide wan space
   To come slanting back with the spear-white
      harpstring rain.

VALIANT FLYER OF THE AIR

An Effusion in Free Rhyme (To Marion Davies)

I

A quiver   a shiver
With one bound
Free of the ground
Up   off   away
   To keep an appointment
   An anointment
   With the sunrise flare
   In silences of the upper air!
A swift climb   a steady lift
Above   beyond familiar nooks and knolls
Where the earth expands   unfolds   unrolls
   Under dauntless wings –

Vista of garden and field   tier on tier
Homesteads   hillbeds and running streams
   Like thoughts chasing each other
   Fly by like the past in dreams –
   The argent spears of a new day's birth
   Pierce blazing across the crust of the earth:
Old earth tossing and pitching
      In quaint curved motion
         Like rolls and swells
            Of the stormy ocean –
               Each shift the eclipse
                  Of a new ellipse –

All hail   valiant flyer of the air
Conquistador of time and space
Master of a champion pace
Blotting out distance   forging into rhyme
Disparities of continents and climes
    High in the air you stand
      An eagle careering
        Domineering the blue
          Ready to plunge or soar
          From the old to the new
   – with sunlight sparkle on wings like dew –

  Propeller and motor throb and thunder
  A song of victory and wonder
    On you conqueror trip
      As you leap and dip
        Cleave and sweep
          The vastnesses of space –

  The race through the clouds
    Up towards the sun
      Has begun   is on!

II

      Good speed   speed well!
      Wending your flight towards
        Horizons far unending
         – Lost in the overhead blaze
         – A mere speck in the haze
    Now no longer visible to the eye

Our mundane show
But a color blur
A raised chart
Patches   snatches of nameless hue
That melt from view –

Entangled in eddies of some wild gust
Away from low clouds and blue rain dust
    Where white mists ensheath
    The plane like a cloak of fleece
    As it dives   on vaporous wave
    Into a giant cumulus cave
With walls ever crumbling – or is it chaos?
      Phantom shapes piling up
       Toppling and tumbling
    Into palace stairs   enchanted aisles
    Dream arcades and balustrades
    Temple ruins on some mountain
  Opalescent as a fairy fountain
  Breaking mingling iridescence –

    Immune to wants   fatigue and cold
    Pilot   unfaltering   bold
    Onward you sail to a sky
    Where above the winds you fly –

Bird of passage   go on beating the dusk of eve
  As league long sunbeams flee
Over the sunken brine of a vanished sea
To paint the range from crest to timberline
    Crimson like wild young wine –

Caught by the pursuing shade of earth
A welcome to damp lampblack night
    With its circling swing
        Of the Milky Way aflame
        And bright constellations
            Dancing and prancing
    To the pulsations of the plane
            And there balancing
    Over a city's nocturnal glow
    The fiery script of stars
        In the sable flow
        Seems to glitter
    From heavens above and below –

    Afloat in splendid space
    Above cloudland dome and tower
        You bloom forth like a skyflower
Straining towards the eastern light
Until your winged petals with dawn turn white!

III
        Alone in the azure –
        No sound of surf
        No forest moan
        No human voice near –
        Onward   Upward! Have no fear!

This is the hour to do and dare
All that lies deep in man astir
All passions of youth a-whir
    Hippidiehip heigho!
      Higher and higher
        Nigher and nigher
        To the limitless waste
        (non-Euclidean
        If that is the taste)
Below the sleeping world of things
Beyond the cosmic sea of stellar dust
    Mounting   wooing
     Scaling   subduing
       With deafening roar
         Like a whip that cracks
    Skimming along the edge
    The uneven ledge
    Of our planet atmosphere
    The naked shore
    Where the feel of other worlds
     Chills the breath –

    Heigho Hippidehip!
     A bold salute
       To the absolute
        To God   and all deities
        That on this globe have trod
     A challenge that soon
     There will be superior journeys
      To mars and moon!

Intermezzo:

Soon the highways midst the byways of the sky
Will turn gray as if darkened by the sway of
Birds migrating southward far away –

Gone also the glamor of steamer and train   wonders
Of another age – what seemed a priceless dower the
Whirlwind of these flying hordes is robbing of its
Power –

And the wise men whose hangars smile on the hills
With banners unfurled are like knights of old the
Rulers of this world –

(play this pianissimo on piccolo and saxophone)

IV

      Icarus   son of Daedalus
      Your foolhardy flight of yore
      To which brave men of before
        With hearts on fire
        Did aspire
        Is done   won
      The conquest of the universe is on –

      Why all this splurge
        This hustle and urge
          To get quicker from place to place
            For what is the search!

Just a journey from some emerald lawn
    To a silver dawn!
      Just another triumph of brain over matter?
      Or do thereby   human ills shatter
        Old superstitions scatter
          Will it glean a golden mean
          Yield a sense of growing stronger
            Day by day
        By inherent powers
        On the soul's new day!

Oh time could we but read in thy uncut
    Pages of man's achievements in the fiery
    Flux of flying ages!

(1900)

DOLOR[*]

I had a deep-red sorrow
  That stained my face with tears;
There loomed no bright to-morrow
  Through all the serried years.
What most I loved had vanished
  And love itself seemed slain;
The wine of life was banished
  For the bitter lees of pain.
  I thought this was the sorrow,
  As deep as man may know,
  For which there is no morrow
  When life regains its glow;
  That time could not dismember
  Grim visions of regret,
  That love would still remember,
  That love could not forget.

And now I brood in silence,
  My eyes are drained of tears;
My dreams, like futile islands,
  Drift on a sea of fears.
Were ashes by some dismal hand
  Whirled o'er memory's plain,
And sorrow tossed to the silent land
  Which knows not love nor pain!
  This is the deepest sorrow
  That man may ever know:
  There is a bright to-morrow
  For every human woe;

[*] Lines suggested by Eduard Steichen's print 'Dolor.'

173

That time can well dismember
All visions of regret,
That love can not remember,
That love will soon forget.

(1903)

A MONOLOGUE

Scene: Fifth Avenue, between Thirtieth and Thirty-first Streets. Enter Hamlet-Steichen, wearing a Japanese obi as a necktie.

To paint or photograph – that is the question:
Whether 'tis more to my advantage to color
Photographic accidents and call them paintings,
Or squeeze the bulb against a sea of critics
And by exposure kill them? To paint – to 'snap':–
No more; and, by a snap, to say we end
The heartache, and the thousand natural shocks
That art is heir to – 'tis a consummation
Devoutly to be wish'd. To paint – to snap;
Perchance to tell the truth:– aye! there's the rub.
How may a fact be lost in fuzziness
When we have cast aside the painter's brush
Must give us pause: There's the respect
That makes picture-painting of so long life;
For who would bear the whips and scorns of time,
The dealer's wrong, the patron's proud contumely,
The pangs of despised art, the cash's delay,
The 'nerve' of the profession, and the spurns
That patient merit of the unworthy takes,
When he himself might triumph over all
With a base camera? Who would brushes clean?
To grunt and sweat in schools or studios,
But that photograms were not dependent
On some manual fake: Photography turned painting;
Paintographs or photopaints; a sad plight,
Which makes me rather bear (at times) the painter's ills
Than turn entirely secessionist.

Thus prudence makes chameleons of us all;
And thus my native store of 'faky' talents
Is sicklied o'er with scarcity of tricks;
And enterprises of great moment to A.S.,
With this regard, their currents turn awry
And lose the name: artistic. Soft you now!
The Käsebier, austere, comes down the street. Nymph of Newport,
In thy brownish tints be all my sins remembered!

(1903)

TO A.T.[*]

What lives in me yet
   ('I died so long ago')
Is merely a thought of you
    That once was oriflame and victory true

All else I forgot:
   All we have been, rapture and dream,
Turned to sand-drifts, wind shifts,
   Desert pictures mistily seen

Like a faded leaf, gold dust agleam,
   Like a book long lost, its thoughts astream;
       Like a face I knew
       But cannot recall,
       Like a song of youth
       That meant life and all,

Only one thought of you
   Could not be touched by death,
It is still throbbing within me
   As some wind's vague warm breath.

(1923)

[*] Anne Throop (1869–??)

177

SNOWFALL

Monotonous, frail flakes are descending,
Feathers from cloud pillows drifting down,
A mist-veil gray heaven is sending
To cover life in field and town.

Feathers from cloud pillows drifting down
As daylight starts to falter and wane,
To cover all life in field and town
Like sleep relieving the body's strain.

As daylight starts to falter and wane,
White foliage, falling soft and faint,
Like sleep redeeming the body's strain
Your frost leaves conquer all earthborn taint.

White foliage falling soft and faint
From what frozen forest do you hail
Mist flakes blurring all earthworn taint –
Vague journeys of the heart that leave no trail!

From what dank gaunt region do you hail
Pale ember sparks from memory's crest –
Dim journeys of heart-rime that left no trail –
Strewing the present with deepest rest!

Sky jewels scattered from memory's crest,
Infinite patterns of spectral wear
Strewing the present with lethean rest
Why are you crowding the ashen air!

Infinite patterns of spectral wear
Placid and bright in your feathery flight
Why do you sport the ashen air
And turn this world so silent and white!

Snow ghosts, star hosts, in feathery flight,
Globe crystals, summoned to break without pain
Burying all life in field and town –
Do you fleck and streak the ashen air
To impart to storm voids some argent refrain
By painting this world so silent and white!

(1927)

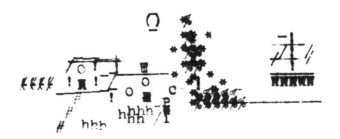

the shepherd leadeth home his flock of hh
the moon rises over the ramshackle buildings
the ship rocketh on the water

(1931)

* Hartmann included this 'typewriter designing' in a letter to his nineteen-year-old daughter Wistaria on March 20, 1931. This example melds Hartmann's interests in visual and verbal art, however glibly. (From the holdings of Special Collections & University Archives, UCR Library, University of California, Riverside)

OBITUARY

The old Mission bells are ringing!   Sadakichi Hartmann is dying!
the old mission bells   unrung for ages   are vibrating in tune
on their own chord: Sadakichi Hartmann is dying   just a scene-
shift   the lost record of some lay   in a mystery play   From Nowhere
To Naught   words leave no trace   whether uttered by extra or star
few thoughts are on par

   The gulls are a-flutter   the sun is aflame   white clouds clut-
   ter and build a form-world that puts art to shame   the old Mission bells with many a clang and clank try to outclamor the
   breaker's   roar   the crush of the waves against the shore
   foam banners are flying   Sadakichi is dying

Big 'tinkling Anne'   astir with the past   clear carillons of Flanders   where she was cast   her hour has come   she breaks loose from
the rafter   and as in a grave disaster   shoots down with a clattering clash   a sentence broken closed with a dash   most folks are
dead before they die   still alive to beloved ones   to others it does
not matter much whether they were ever there or not.

   The wind sweeps in form oversea   ha ha haws* at the bells
   and makes them ring and sing and swing with a wider fling:
   Sadakichi Hartmann is dying NOW   dissonance reigns   a riot
   of strains: most of life spells insanity   the remainder is
   vanity   nobody cares   nobody dares   wars unroll   youth pays
   the toll   empires rise   pass away   poverty prevails   disease
   has its sway   Nature stays   the human race decays

---

* Hartmann explains: 'referring to Sadakichi's famous laugh which still must haunt forgotten gath-
ering places in the Village, on Russian Hill and the left bank of the Seine (*Washington Evening Star*,
June 1937).'

181

abuse of Force is the cause of all perturbation
does death hold a secret and revelation?

The old Mission bells have no answer   they shiver and toss   they
whimper and weep   as they woo sleep   hush!   Sadakichi Hartmann
is gone   a new scene is on
      sounds like flowers drop one by one

      Bing! Bang! Bung! Bing! Bong!
      Bung! Bing! Bing! Bong! Bang!

(1943–44)

During his lifetime, Hartmann published poems in little magazines and self-published four of his own books – each several times and in different editions. Edwin Markam, the editor of the 1910 anthology *The Younger Choir*, included Hartmann as one of the rising poets of the early twentieth century. More recently, Hartmann's poetry has been anthologized in David Hsin-Fu Wand's *Asian American Heritage: An Anthology of Prose and Poetry*, Juliana Chang's *Quiet Fire: A Historical Anthology of Asian American Poetry*, Cary Nelson's *Anthology of Modern American Poetry*, Stephen Gould Axelrod et al's *New Anthology of American Poetry*, and Robert Hass's *American Poetry: The Twentieth Century*. In his review of the latter, critic Allan Burns calls Hartmann one of the 'missing links' of American poetry.[41]

Thanks to recovery efforts by George Knox, Jane Calhoun Weaver, and others, Hartmann's reputation as a bon vivant and art critic is secure. David Hsin-Fu Wand and Juliana Chang, however, deserve credit for calling attention to his poetry and naming him an 'Asian American' – a term that was born long after Hartmann died. In his 1974 anthology, Wand argues that Hartmann 'deserves mention as a pioneering voice in Asian American literature.' Valorizing his resistance to being interned during the Second World War, Wand maintains, 'It is his ethnic consciousness, rather than his occasional poetry, that makes him contemporary in spirit and acceptable to the majority of postwar Asian American poets, who are concerned with the rediscovery of their ethnic heritage.'[42] In Chang's 1996 anthology, Hartmann receives pride of place. She writes, 'Asian American poetry dates as far back as the 1890s, with the publication of poems by Sadakichi Hartmann, considered among the first to write Symbolist poetry in English.'[43] A review of which poems they chose to include in their anthologies suggests that Wand prioritized Hartmann's connection to his Japanese heritage while Chang was more open to the range of his poetic achievements.

In contrast, the influential editors of the 1974 anthology *Aiiieeeee!* rejected Hartmann altogether. They argue the following:

The tradition of Japanese American verse as being quaint and foreign in English, established by Yone Noguchi and Sadakichi Hartman [*sic*], momentarily influenced American writing with the quaintness of the Orient but said nothing about Asian America, because, in fact, these writers weren't Asian Americans but Americanized Asians.[44]

What are we to make of this rejection? In some ways, their refusal to acknowledge Hartmann parallels their refusal to acknowledge another multiracial writer who has since become a subject of intense study: Onoto Watanna, née Winnifred Eaton. Born of an English father and Chinese mother, Eaton adopted a Japanese-sounding pseudonym to pursue a career as a writer. She even made up a Japanese signature, claimed to be born in Nagasaki, and dressed in a kimono for publicity photographs. This persona helped Eaton to sell many novels and even become a chief scenarist for a Hollywood studio. Some critics accuse her of passing as Japanese merely to appeal to the turn-of-the-century taste for *Japonisme* and make money. More recently, however, other critics have read greater subtlety and even subversion in her work.[45]

What might Eaton's literary critical history portend for Hartmann? He made similar choices in self-presentation but only sometimes and not necessarily for profit. In addition, Hartmann cultivated many other literary and artistic personae from the buttoned-down Sidney Allan of *Camera Work* to the anti-war Sadakichi Hartmann of *My Rubaiyat*. In a poem entitled 'Monologue', Hartmann's speaker announces, 'prudence makes chameleons of us all'. But prudence alone is not the reason behind Hartmann's plural aspects and performances. Regarding the supposed connection between one's heritage and one's art he wrote, 'Biographical data do not interest me. What is the difference where a man is born, how old he is, where he studied, and where he was medaled? His art must speak – that is all I care for.'[46] Certainly critics will debate the political meanings of Hartmann's self-presentation and his choice of literary subjects and forms, but in the end his art must speak. With this first ever edition of his collected poems in English, we are in a better position to listen.[47]

ACKNOWLEDGEMENTS

Wistaria Linton deserves special recognition for preserving her father's manuscripts, which now reside in the Sadakichi Hartmann Papers in the Special Collections of the University of California Riverside. For providing access to archival material, I would like to thank the professional and gracious staff members of the Special Collections at the University of California Riverside, the Rauner Special Collections Library at Dartmouth College, and the Mortimer Rare Book Room at Smith College. For providing research assistance, I would like to thank Rachel Foster. Thanks go also to Andrew Latimer and Jessica Kelly of Little Island Press for guiding this volume through the publication process; the Smith College Committee on Faculty Compensation and Development for funding portions of my research; my colleagues at Smith College and the Five College Asian/Pacific/American Studies Program for encouraging my work; Miliann Kang for helping me polish the introduction; Claire Cheung for assisting with the index; and Sheri Cheung for being my first and best reader.

ENDNOTES

1. This introduction to Hartmann's poetry builds on the literary critical work of Gerald Haslam, 'Three Exotics: Yone Noguchi, Shiesei Tsuneishi, and Sadakichi Hartmann,' *CLA Journal* 19 (1976): pp. 362–373; Marshall Van Deusen, 'Sadakichi Hartmann,' *Dictionary of Literary Biography,* vol. 54 (Detroit: Gale, 1987), pp. 154–63; Deckard Francis Hodge, 'Expatriate Modernisms: Border Crossing in the 1920s,' Ph.D. diss., University of California, Riverside, 2005; Merton Lee, 'Asian American Poetry, American Poetry, and the Critique of Identity: Asian American Poetry in Comparative Context, 1887–2005,' Ph.D. diss., University of Illinois at Urbana-Champaign, 2012; and Audrey Wu Clark, The Asian American Avant-Garde (Philadelphia: Temple University Press, 2015), ch. 2. For discussions of Hartmann as an art critic, see Jane Calhoun Weaver, *Sadakichi Hartmann: Critical Modernist* (Berkeley: University of California Press, 1991) and Lauren Kroiz, *Creative Composites: Modernism, Race, and the Stieglitz Circle* (Berkeley: University of California Press, 2012). For his own account of his perfume concerts, see Hartmann, 'In Perfume Land,' *Forum* (Aug. 1913): 217–228. For accounts of his drinking, see Gene Fowler, *Minutes of the Last Meeting* (New York: Viking Press, 1954) and Hartmann, *White Chrysanthemums: Literary Fragments and Pronouncements,* edited by George Knox and Harry Lawton (New York: Herder and Herder, 1971), p. 31.
2. John Barrymore qtd. in Fowler, p. 7.
3. Hartmann's early publisher, Guido Bruno, may have been the best at this describing him as 'the son of a German father and a Japanese mother, a burgomaster's son from Mecklenburg, the only European state without a Constitution, and the daughter of a ronin, a roving soldier of Old Japan' (advertisement for the Bruno Chap Book edition of *Tanka and Haikai*). Notably, this description predicts Hartmann's literary independence by highlighting or maybe even concocting the political independence of his parents' origins.
4. Qtd. in Kroiz. p. 15. Thomas Christensen also has noted that 'in many ways he was plural' in *River of Ink: Literature, History, and Art* (Berkeley: Counterpoint Press, 2014), p. 355.
5. According to Andrew Way Leong, it is strictly incorrect to say that Hartmann was Japanese German because the status of both nations was in flux in 1867. See his chapter in progress, 'Unequal Entreaties: Sadakichi Hartmann's *Conversations with Walt Whitman* (1895)'. Hartmann's daughter Atma claims that Osada was the daughter of Kunisada, a famous artist, in a letter she wrote in Oct., 1925, but this cannot be substantiated by Kunisada's biography (box 118, Sadakichi Hartmann Papers, Special Collections of the University of California, Riverside).
6. Hartmann wrote, 'I knew Jean Valjean much better than my venerable father who seldom honored my childhood with his presence' in *White Chrysanthemums,* p. 155.
7. 'To Walt Whitman'.
8. On the phenomenon of older white male poets' literary and social interactions with younger poets of Japanese ancestry, see Amy Suyematsu, *Queer Compulsions: Race, Nation, and Sexuality in the Affairs of Yone Noguchi* (Honolulu: University of Hawai'i Press, 2012). It is also notable that Whitman bequeathed his personal copy of the 1875 edition of *Leaves of Grass* to Hartmann, which now resides at Michigan State University's Special Collections Library.
9. George Knox and Harry Lawton, Introduction, *The Whitman-Hartmann Controversy* (Bern: Herbert Lang, 1976), pp. 44–45.

10. Walt Whitman, 'Song of Myself,' *Walt Whitman's* Leaves of Grass *and Other Writings,* ed. Michael Moon (New York: Norton, 2002), pp. 77, 78.

11. Hartmann, 'The Japanese Conception of Poetry,' *Reader Magazine,* 3 (January 1904): p. 189.

12. Interestingly, Hartmann lists his previous nationality as German in his naturalization papers, perhaps to avoid the possible complications of being born in an Asian nation. By 1892, Congress had renewed the Chinese Exclusion Act of 1882, which prohibited the Chinese immigrants from applying for naturalized citizenship. Although this did not apply to Japanese immigrants, perhaps Hartmann was able to see the writing on the wall. In the coming years, the Congress passed the Asiatic Barred Zone Act of 1917 and the Immigration Act of 1924, as well as various laws that prohibited Japanese from owning land. His place of birth is listed as Japan, however, in the 1900 census report.

13. Whitman, 'As I Ebb'd with the Ocean of Life', *Leaves,* p. 213.

14. Kirsten Blythe Painter, *Flint on a Bright Stone: A Revolution of Precision and Restraint in American, Russian, and German Modernism* (Stanford: Stanford University Press, 2006), p. 20.

15. Painter, p. 16.

16. Hartmann, *Passport to Immortality* (Beaumont, CA: Hartmann), p. 10.

17. Hartmann, 'In Perfume Land,' *Forum* (Aug. 1913): p. 217.

18. Weaver, p. 1. Weaver collects much of Hartmann's art criticism in *Sadakichi Hartmann: Critical Modernist.*

19. Hartmann, 'On the Vanity of Appreciation,' *Camera Work* 5 (Jan. 1904): p. 23.

20. He sired seven more children with his second wife Lillian Bonham and one more child with his lover Ann Throop.

21. Hartmann, 'Eduard J. Steichen, Painter-Photographer,' in Weaver, pp. 304–5.

22. Hartmann, *Passport,* p. 29.

23. *White Chrysanthemums,* p. 31.

24. Guido Bruno et al., 'Notes on Hartmann,' *Greenwich Village* 3 (Nov. 1915): 7–10+; Richard Hill, 'The First Hippie,' *Swank International* 16 (1969): p. 16–18.

25. Hartmann, 'A Plea for the Picturesqueness of New York,' *Camera Notes* (1 Oct. 1900): 91–97.

26. Edward FitzGerald, *Rubaiyat of Omar Khayyam in English Verse* (New York: Houghton, 1902), p. 58.

27. John Roger Paas, 'Under Omar's Subtle Spell: American Reprint Publishers and the Omar Craze,' in *Fitzgerald's Rubaiyat of Omar Khayyam: Popularity and Neglect*, edited by Adrian Poole et al. (New York: Anthem Press, 2011), p. 132.

28. Critic Gerald W. Haslam argues that this passage comes 'dangerously close to the pathetic fallacy' in 'Three Exotics: Yone Noguchi, Shiesei Tsuneishi, and Sadakichi Hartmann,' *CLA Journal* 19 (1976): p. 371.

29. Hartmann, *Permanent Peace: Is it a Dream?* (New York: Bruno, 1915), p. 55.

30. Axelrod et al, p. 671.

31. Hodge, p. 162.

32. Ibid., p. 161.

33. Allan Burns, 'Reinventing American Poetry,' *Papers on Language and Literature* 4 (2000): p. 437.

34. Qtd. in Painter, p. 88.

35. Ce Rosenow, 'Fenollosa's Legacy: The Japanese Network of Ezra Pound,' *Philological Quarterly* 3–4 (2006): p. 381.

36. 'The Japanese Conception of Poetry,' p. 189.

37. Ibid. Evidently, the Japanese did not share the Western notion of the pathetic fallacy.

38. 'Vanity of Appreciation'.

39. *White Chrysanthemums*, p. 140.

40. Ibid., p. 20.

41. Burns, 'Reinventing,' p. 437.

42. Wand, p. 127. His resistance to internment is an overstatement according to Hartmann's FBI file, which reveals that he inquired about moving east to live with one of his daughters but was ultimately deemed too much of an 'invalid' with no history of 'subversive activities' to bother interning. Of course, he still faced occasional harassment from locals but not from the federal government.

43. Juliana Chang, ed., *Quiet Fire: A Historical Anthology of Asian American Poetry, 1892–1970* (New York: Asian American Writers Workshop, 1996), p. xvi.

44. Frank Chin et al., *Aiiieeeee!: An Anthology of Asian American Writers* (Washington, DC: Howard University Press, 1974), p. xv.

45. See Dominika Ferens, 'Winnifred Eaton/Onoto Watanna: Establishing Ethnographic Authority,' in *Form and Transformation in Asian American Literature*, ed. Zhou Xiaojing and Samina Najmi (Seattle: University of Washington Press, 2005): pp. 30–47.

46. Hartmann, 'A Visit to Steichen's Studio,' *Camera Work* 2 (April 1903): p. 25.

47. Saburō Ōta published a Japanese translation of most but not all of Hartmann's poems in *Hangyaku no geijutsuka: sekai no bohemian = Sadakichi no shōgai* (Tokyo: Tokyo Bijutsu, 1972).

INDEX OF POEM TITLES